PARAGON PARK

PARAGON PARK

Turtle, Swan

Bethlehem in Broad Daylight

Early Poems

MARK DOTY

DAVID R. GODINE · *Publisher*
Boston

First published in 2012 by
DAVID R. GODINE · *Publisher*
Post Office Box 450
Jaffrey, New Hampshire 03452
www.godine.com

LIBRARY OF CONGRESS CATALOGING-IN-PUBLICATION DATA

Doty, Mark.
Paragon park : Turtle swan, Bethlehem in broad daylight, early poems :
poems / by Mark Doty. — 1st U.S. ed.
p.   cm.
Includes bibliographical references and index.
ISBN 978-1-56792-442-8 (alk. paper)
PS3554.O798P37   2012
811'.54—dc23
2011035967

FIRST EDITION
Printed in the United States of America

Contents

Turtle, Swan

Bethlehem in Broad Daylight

Early Poems

TURTLE, SWAN

For Wally

A Replica of the Parthenon

One of my presents, one Christmas,
was a *Golden Treasury of Archaeology*,
a book too big for my hands,
its cover illustrated with masks from Sumer
and a terraced ziggurat. The book was heavy enough
to suggest it contained a secret weight,
and I stared and dreamed, sure that some subtext
buried, like foundations, would come clear.
Heinrich Schliemann unearthed seven cities,
one atop the other; time lines graphed them
layer by layer. Everywhere
the unsuspected lay beneath the earth.

In a neighbor girl's front yard we played
the same game every one of the summer twilights,
blue as Egyptian porcelain, that stretched
between supper and time to come in.
We took turns dying. One would lie down
while the other folded the corpse's hands
and, with the true solemnity of children,
brought flowers. At my grandmother's funeral
the family had been called to come forward
to the casket, her shroud
the same lavender as the little flowers
in her print dresses. I did not know
how I should stand. In her empty bedroom
I made paper ships – a *Niña*,
a *Pinta*, a *Santa Maria* – and sailed them
across the mahogany of her dresser

whose drawers smelled for years
of peppermint and cough drops. I don't know
how my friend knew about dying;
her grandmother still lived in her house,
contained in a front room
where she could watch us from a window.
As blue deepened like heaven descending,
the survivor would begin to pray
while the other could, without moving,
go on toward Paradise. Jesus stood
in the drifting blue, milky and blonde.
He said, "Come in, Mark," or only stood,
bent slightly, listening, as I imagined he did
in the song, "I come to the garden alone,
while the dew is still on the roses . . ."
"My grandmother," my friend said one evening,
"says we can't play. It might come true."

Some Sundays, for an outing, my parents
would take me to a city park, to a replica
of the Parthenon. I recognized it
from the *Golden Treasury*, though the roof
and pediments should have been missing;
it was strange in its completeness.
Inside, fragments of horses – copies –
threw off the odor of damp marble.
Its lesson: that any replacement fails,
and greater artifice only recalls
the original further. I did not think of it

for twenty-five years, recalling the smell
of the book of archaeology and the chilly manes
of the horses, their troubling, twisted necks –
but that replica was also signpost
toward a way of understanding,
a psychology, if you can call it that,
founded not on the minor issues
of sex but on the real terms of loss.
We know that we will lie down
in our own bodies and someone will fold our hands,
and perhaps we will be moving
although we are still. It might come true
of whatever we love or create
to replace what we love. There are buried cities,
one beneath the other. From the first loss,
we begin naming.

This was in Nashville, in 1957.

Latin Dances

My father writes from Arizona:
two weeks rain, longest in memory,
broke an earthen dam in the foothills.
Four feet above ground, his Airsteam
was the center of an island. "There's nothing to do
in the garden or orchard till February."
Always distant, he's used labor
as disguise. I picture him pacing,
restless as ever, the rows of skinny pecans
in his new grove. Over days
the surrounding sheet of water perked down,
left the desert an unexpected cinnabar.
"We found a trout in the road," he writes.
"We have a tape cassette on Spanish
  and I've been spending an hour a day
  listening. Also we have an Arthur Murray record
  on latin dances. We do a fair samba,
  box-step and tango, but flunk out on the mambo.
  Could you find instructions in a bookstore?
  Also we need a good cha – cha." Fish in the chaparral
don't surprise more than this sudden flaring
of small festivities – at seventy the man
who held himself so far away
he seemed hazy and remote as foothills
now throws my stepmother across the trailer floor
in a "fair tango." Chairwoman
of the County Bell Collectors' Society,
President of the District Homemakers –
whose headquarters, the letter goes on,

are now under two feet of mud,
needlework and recipe files sodden with rain
and the occasional lost minnow – does she pin
a plastic rose in her chignon
while he whirls her in circles growing
closer and closer to the shining windows,
rocking the foundations of the trailer? Which stands,
in the flood that's decked the desert
in speckled trout, given to my father
and stepmother's arms and boxstepping feet
the rhythmic and reeling pleasures of survivors.

Rocket

In Iowa, 1971, I wore my hair
in a ponytail nearly to my waist and worked
in a day-care center, passing the time
with children. I took my job seriously;

mornings the old Mercury wouldn't start
I'd walk the steep Twenty-eighth Street hill
to the down-at-heels house
with its front yard full of playground,

remnants of the decades when the school
was Miss Dell's and the children
were divided into Brownies and Fairies,
and once a year in an Easter pageant

the Fairies recited verse while the Brownies
danced in rings. When we cleaned the building out,
the new owners and I, just after Miss Dell
retired into a high-rise for the elderly,

we found programs from thirty years' commencements,
and the waiting lists where every wealthy family
in town registered their child at birth, all decorated
with Miss Dell's watercolors of mushrooms

and jaunty daffodils. She'd single-handedly
passed an Edwardian childhood on to generations.
Some friends at the university, my age or older,
remembered the same playground equipment

as totems of their own childhoods –
the rusty metal rocket, the sandbox
with its promises of discovery and burial.
Detail redeems memory: even an uncertain time,

a poor one, yields at least the tangle
of bittersweet over the grid of fence,
the boundary of the lot where I'd watch
the children. Watch was mostly all I knew

to do, or play. There was a boy I loved
especially, John; somewhere
I have a photograph of me reading to him,
my hair spilling onto his narrow

four-year-old's shoulders,
his face rapt, dreaming into the book.
He wanted nothing of the other teachers,
only to talk to me, and sometimes

for me to lift him to the highest
landing of the rocket four times
his height. It was a kind
of vague intrusion, late in the day,

when his parents came to pick him up.
I was nineteen then, those smoky afternoons
bending into winter, and it was still
a little hard to let him go.

I drove by their house once, on Ingersoll,
an expensive street. The patterned brick,
the striped awnings, pots of pink geraniums –
emblems entirely predictable, nothing

out of place, and his parents' concerns
were correct: the language their son brought home
from school, his clinging to me, his chain of colds
and flus. I'm not sure if I wanted to steal

their child or be him, at the center
of an excellent house,
incapable of faltering . . .
Though I believed surely

the apparent perfection of their lives,
the grace in which they drove their son home
in a clean car – was only an image
above some rift, the seam of darkness

any family must contain. I used to call my mother,
weekends, and it would take my father
a long time to bring her to the phone,
as if he were pulling her from the past

as well as from bed. Once she had just
been talking to the dead, and my father
must have stood by, patient,
while she told me what they had told her,

and when she hung up he must have led her
back into the dimmed room where the ghosts
still gathered, they who had missed her
so long, they who'd brought brushes

and combs for her long hair. John must be what,
now, eighteen? And probably does not remember
the day-care center at all, unless
in some vague way, or unless he lives

there still, in Des Moines, and drives sometimes
by the playground with its red and white rocket
that, for the children, towered over everything.
See, I assume it is still there – and if so

perhaps strikes him now, as we say
things magnified in memory do, as smaller
than he remembered, less dangerous.

In the Form of Snow

The summer I turned eighteen I worked
my first job, night shift in a laundry
and dry cleaning plant. I lugged
the black watchman's clock from room

to room, swept the trash
out from behind trouser presses
and pleating machines and the huge bins
of soap like cylindrical snowdrifts.

The Chicano kid who went home at midnight
told me ghost stories, how the plant was built
over the wash where La Llorona walked,
the mourning woman lost in lament

and a dark rebozo, crying for her children
who'd never come home. I was alone
from twelve to seven, always
something to make noise:

falling coat hangers,
one of the big drum washers
turning a little as if shifting in its sleep,
and once the boss came in at one

and called me over the intercom –
my name, amplified, booming
through those unlit rooms –
to accuse me of stealing a shirt.

At dawn, under a moon
like a nickel gone through the wash,
I'd walk the fourteen blocks home
through the stucco houses and storefronts

to the white apartment, flanked by oleanders
on University Avenue, to my new wife.
Most mornings I only fell asleep;
sometimes she would be up counting

her calendar of yellow pills,
or reading a novel. We didn't know then,
though maybe anyone around us could have said,
what we'd come to – grief and anger

that would seep into everything like a dye.
We were more worried about how to buy
an air conditioner for the bedroom
that looked out onto the city clock

blinking the hour, and what to say,
and about the small cluster of blood that had loosed
from her body like a traveling star
and might have been our child.

We didn't, as my mother said, know shit –
much less, afterward, how we'd learn
to get over it. Loss you can imagine
before the fact, but forgetting . . .

What seems most real to me now is the smell
of the solvent they used to clean stains,
how it seeped into my collars and sleeves,
and nothing we could do would take it out.

The snow this morning
comes in great casual gusts
and then scatters into separate motions,
single flakes that have made me think

of the laundry, and of the color
of the stolen shirt. These flakes
could fall anywhere, and do,
or don't – some seem to blow on

to nowhere we can conceive. Though some settle,
and the fact of this taking place
seems miraculous, because anything
could have happened, and this did.

La Belle et la Bête

"My heart," he said, "is the heart
of a beast." What could she do
but love him? First she must resist:
the copper bowls gleaming on the rack

in her father's kitchen, the white bloom
of the basin, the good ladle that remained in place
hadn't promised her this. There
the lamps had required her hand to light them,

the mirrors were plain and dependable
as laundry. Trading herself for a rose,
a single red gesture, she'd arrived
at this vague castle where the glass

said "I am your mirror, *la belle*,"
and showed her a clouded double,
almost a ghost. Where were her simple objects
of affection now? The Beast steamed

with the thrill of a slaughtered doe.
His ruined garden – haze formed into hedge
and topiary – smoked, the grottoes
infinite and intimate at once.

Even the statuary watched,
as if to cautiously urge her on; for them
there were no secrets,
no future to reel out its flickering patterns

of light and dark. So Beauty does
as she does: these cautious walks with the Beast,
at first tentative, her skirt scraping
like cicadas against the marble,

then her hand in his glove. His rough paws
produce for her an Oceania of pearls;
she wears them across her bodice as though
she'd keep everything of his at the surface,

somewhere above her heart.
Of course she loves him wholly, in the end,
although it does not appear wise to do so,
which transforms his wolfish muzzle

into the bland and pretty face of a prince.
But it's not him anyone remembers –
rather the heady onrush
of the transformation, the will

that eventually unfurls the body
beneath the fur. The moments,
disruptive and lush, before the breaking through –
the power to bloom

through solid walls,
not to the kingdom itself, where nothing happens,
but the approach to the kingdom:
everything, the coming to love.

Turtle, Swan

Because the road to our house
is a back road, meadowlands punctuated
by gravel quarry and lumberyard,
there are unexpected travelers
some nights on our way home from work.
Once, on the lawn of the Tool

and Die Company, a swan;
the word doesn't convey the shock
of the thing, white architecture
rippling like a pond's rain – pocked skin,
beak lifting to hiss at my approach.
Magisterial, set down in elegant authority,

he let us know exactly how close we might come.
After a week of long rains
that filled the marsh until it poured
across the road to make in low woods
a new heaven for toads,
a snapping turtle lumbered down the center

of the asphalt like an ambulatory helmet.
His long tail dragged, blunt head jutting out
of the lapidary prehistoric sleep of shell.
We'd have lifted him from the road
but thought he might bend his long neck back
to snap. I tried herding him; he rushed,

though we didn't think those blocky legs
could hurry – then ambled back
to the center of the road, a target
for kids who'd delight in the crush
of something slow with the look
of primeval invulnerability. He turned

the blunt spear point of his jaws,
puffing his undermouth like a bullfrog,
and snapped at your shoe,
vising a beakful of – thank God –
leather. You had to shake him loose. We left him
to his own devices, talked on the way home

of what must lead him to new marsh
or old home ground. The next day you saw,
one town over, remains of shell
in front of the little liquor store. I argued
it was too far from where we'd seen him,
too small to be his . . . though who could tell

what the day's heat might have taken
from his body. For days he became a stain,
a blotch that could have been merely
oil. I did not want to believe that
was what we saw alive in the firm center
of his authority and right

to walk the center of the road,
head up like a missionary moving certainly
into the country of his hopes.
In the movies in this small town
I stopped for popcorn while you went ahead
to claim seats. When I entered the cool dark

I saw straight couples everywhere,
no single silhouette who might be you.
I walked those two aisles too small
to lose anyone and thought of a book
I read in seventh grade, *Stranger than Science*,
in which a man simply walked away,

at a picnic, and was,
in the act of striding forward
to examine a flower, gone.
By the time the previews ended
I was nearly in tears – then realized
the head of one-half the couple in the first row

was only your leather jacket propped in the seat
that would be mine. I don't think I remember
anything of the first half of the movie.
I don't know what happened to the swan. I read
every week of some man's lover showing
the first symptoms, the night sweat

or casual flu, and then the wasting begins
and the disappearance a day at a time.
I don't know what happened to the swan;
I don't know if the stain on the street
was our turtle or some other. I don't know
where these things we meet and know briefly,

as well as we can or they will let us,
go. I only know that I do not want you
– you with your white and muscular wings
that rise and ripple beneath or above me,
your magnificent neck, eyes the deep mottled
        autumnal colors
of polished tortoise – I do not want you ever to die.

Gardenias

In Puerto Rico in 1939 my mother has leaned
against a garden gate, her hands in the black
dotted pockets of her dress. In one she holds
a small bitter orange she's picked today.
She is waiting for my father, who's perhaps
stopped again for gardenias at the market; his truck
might be mired in this afternoon's rain.
When he does come he will carry beside him
his leather case of tools: level and T square,
compass, a little gray testament of trigonometric functions,
the rolled prints of a bridge, thunderhead blue.
She would like to ride on the seat
beside him, its cracked upholstery cool against
the straight seams of her hose. She watches the road,
pokes a black, strapped heel at the foot
of a clump of lilies blaring their whiteness
above the fence, taller than anything at home.
Here green is magnified, the blooms more headily fragrant
than everything she's known. She would like him
to regard her as he does the tools,
each set in its polished, latched case.
Instead she is part of this garden
and its dense, florid heat, its lack of boundaries,
its insistent green. I will not be conceived
for fourteen years, though perhaps I am in some form
imagined, the outline of "son" like a vacancy
in some unpainted section a muralist
has saved for last, unable to imagine
how the space remaining might be filled.

She may imagine the nimbus forms of my sister,
my shadow brother who'll die at birth.
(She will tell me where he's buried,
but I cannot remember.) What I can construct
of this scene rises from snapshots and the recollection
of snapshots. For the moment's dreamed duration,
this is the height of summer, the southern cross
already rising, not yet visible, behind the deep blue rim
of the afternoon's storm. She stands with her back
to the garden of melons and rampant mint,
dizzy as if overpowered by perfume, and leans
into the gatepost with all her weight,
her eyes closed, waiting into evening
for the truck grinding gravel at the foot of the hill.

Horses

The nights were blue and star-regular as church.
Ponies bit at the paint on the Chevrolet.

From the rope swing I watched their rambling lives
my mother said had nothing to do with ours.

That year we lived in a house with no insides;
I watched the white porch from the foot of the hill,

dark rectangles of windows, a tangle
of trumpet vine near the lattice.

Another year the house was all
screened veranda filled with my father's voice

when he spanked me, hands red as his loud face.
Then only a lawn where I dug for marbles,

tracked the drift and rise of fireflies. One house
after another; permanence lay in things,

etched palmettos cut finger-deep
in a round mirror, a chest of drawers

infinite with handkerchiefs and nightgowns
to bury my hands in cool sliding. My mother drank,

painted in oils: even her lilacs redolent of damage,
bruised petals curling in on themselves,

layers of paint so thick they never dried.
My father said *You be her husband*

and disappeared without a word or departure,
a magic act better than limp hares slipped

from hats on Saturday morning TV. Good boy,
I did what I was told, wondered at how large

my job was, how adult. Try as I would
I'd never be able to repair the darkness

that welled from the center of the flowers,
the stalks too heavy to stand, the sickness

that crept even into their perfume.
The good boy in the grade school photograph

has hair darker than mine,
large eyes; the solemn look of guilt

denies the limits of his age.
He is too old. I want to tell him

I almost hear the horses
that filled our landlord's dusty lot,

drifting and hurrying beside the outbuildings
like rainstorms, engines of summer thunder,

the mares roped and carried away in trucks
to give birth, lovely and not ours.

Late Conversation

From the window Twenty-eighth is slick with rain,
the corner shop's displays doubled
and rippling. I imagine you,
student of skies, standing
in the hallway. From the landing
you watch blue as I watch myself –
the way one studies a caged fortune-teller
move her wax palm over cards,
pause over a future . . .
Even after it's eluded us for years,
it's motion we look for in the mirror,
the weather beneath the skin.
I'm content to talk to you
through the barely open door.

> *you there – I here*
> *with just the Door ajar*

Today the slow-witted boy
across the street told me
he hears me typing at night;
how my attic windows must look,
evenings, those low barred frames
glowing down through the crabapple . . .
A child who lived across the road
from your high hedges remembered
your lit blind upstairs, how sometimes
she'd glimpse with a shiver
"Miss Emily's shadow." To others,

undaunted by legend – the apparition
of your white dress moving, afternoons,
in the orchard – you lowered cakes
in a basket tied to a length of rope.
You carried them upstairs,
breathless as ever, from the kitchen
where you kneaded flour
bleached as your sleeves

> *that white Sustenance*
> *Despair*

eggs, butter. Daisy,
you called yourself to a man
who'd always elude you.
A more solitary bloom, I'd say:
white delphinium, calla.
You were no eyeful of sun.

> *but bold, like the chestnut burr –*
> *and my eyes, like the sherry*
> *in the glass that the guest leaves*

and the guests left, one after another,
or else you saw them through a slit
in the door. A few occasions, a few
occasional visitors: a friend from school
whom you offered her choice between a glass
of wine and a rose, a faculty wife

invited to the back stairs "alone,
by moonlight," a seamstress
who spent a week sewing –
bridal gowns, shrouds, baker's uniforms
pure and severe? Your appetite for silence grew,
and the pastry's perfection: silver to stir,
glass to measure – the trochee,
the loved, liberal dash,
the glancing rhyme of pearl
and alcohol exact as cake.
What a lonely circling,
the trade of Circumference!
Once your father rang church bells,
summoned sleepers to view an aurora:
who heard your carillon, all of space
tolling beneath your steady weather?
Shall we discuss a monumental loneliness?
A common attraction to unattainable
objects? till the heart
would choke on it – that bird

small, like the wren

wrapped in such choiring . . .

Split the lark and you'll see the music

or an aversion to silence,
granting us this business:

to encircle. So sing,
shadow in the hall, from behind the door.
I will not open it. No intrusions. Like you,
like stars, I am retreating year by year,
and these rooms seem enough:
midnight to north and south, and the mirror
I study from this bed filled,
in its upper reaches, with
silvered light, vacant.

     – bright Absentee

Like a fontanel, Emily, like a door,
my face, yours, closing.

Nancy Outside in July

after Jim Dine

In these prints, twenty-five variations
on a single plate, the artist has masked his model,
his wife – Nancy – with the grindings of a burr wheel,
with lilies, smears of streaked black paint,
the bent supplications of wild cyclamen:

a study of what is hidden or revealed – sometimes
both – by addition or erasure. Here tulips
the color of a fading bruise loom before a background
so black it seems a pure window of night sky
until one discerns her face. Here she's scrawled

by fauve swoops of paint. Talking in the gallery,
you and I both want to work. You'd draw me, also
in variation; I'd draft a sequence, "Nancy" replaced
by your name: "Wally Outside in July" followed by
Dine's subtitles: "Among Flowers of the Holy Land,"

"Above the Trees." In "Wrestling with Spirits,"
she has been overcome by a deep jay blue
that seems to well out of her own body, obscure
her steady gaze. Behind your face I'd place the image
of your father – the way sometimes I look at you,

working, say, on the old trunk you stripped
and oiled in the strong sunlight of our bedroom window,
and see as if through you to the hovering, other

man. That distant figure is always going, caught
in departure, but indelible, a watermark

unseen until the paper's held to the light
to reveal the distinguishing emblem, no matter what
image is printed over it. Likewise I imagine
you would place behind my body another one,
the hurt son still foolishly loyal

to his father. You'd draw my face tattooed
like your father's arm, the dark ink spreading,
a needlepoint of grief – as if to re-create that mark
in me would somehow release you. It doesn't work,
much as we'd like to believe that false magic.

Although the flowers that cover Nancy's face
in one print are entirely black, blooms
of soft, scorched coal, the "Flowers of the Holy Land"
seem projected from the depths of her eyes;
lilies and cyclamen twine around her mouth

as if shaped from her breath. Although
he paints her dark, the printmaker still forges
her exhalation into a luminous botany,
these burnished leaves won from wrestling
with spirits. After the exhibit, in the lobby

of the Lenox Hotel, the mirrored walls offer
the most familiar image of reflected endlessness.

In the distance of the glass's smaller reaches,
I don't know which of us is which, or care.
This trail of sons enlarges in numbers

as it diminishes. You have my permission:
to draw, to color and discolor, shape
and redefine – just as this, erased
and awkward as it is, spells out nothing
if not your name.

Paragon Park

Across the highway's a city beach;
I've never seen so many radios
and tattoos in one place, and everywhere
the self-conscious strut of teenage boys
parading. But the arcade fronting the sea
is cool, and almost outside of time:
plaster fortune-tellers in glass cages,
machines to test one's strength in love
by the strength of grip. Through the open gates,
spinners and screamers painted
the colors of ice cream, flecked
and peeled by salt air. Roller coaster,
Haunted Palace, the Congo Ride of twenty years ago
become this season's Bermuda Triangle.
The music bounces from loudspeakers –
forties swing suggesting we might see our parents,
freshly stepped from a snapshot, stepping
around the corner; unchanging fragrances
of sea wind, junk food, and the hot gears
of the ferris wheel.

Everyone has his own amusement park;
mine was in Chattanooga, a dusty
and battered place we used to drive to
for hours in the green Studebaker. It seems
we visited a hundred times, though probably
it was only twice. Exhausted by rides,
log chute, spinning top, caterpillar
and the old kind of walk-through fun house

so paralyzed by pleasant fright
I couldn't take another step toward
Dracula's coffin or the kettle of the witch –
then a grassy bank long and green
as June when you are five, lying down
on spread quilts to chicken and lemonade
before fireworks streaked the summer night.

Your parents married when they were sixteen,
and eight kids later they'd load the troop
into a station wagon and drive – on your father's
brief shore leave – once a summer
to Paragon Park. Some morning
you'd wake up and find your father gone again;
they never told you when he was leaving,
out of a will to protect, I guess,
though the lack of knowledge never protected anyone.
And you learned to believe that men
who loved you would never stay,
something you'd later try to prove
– though analysis is easier than the exact memory
of his side of the bed empty on Sunday morning,
his shoes missing from the floor. This afternoon
when we visit your mother she laughs and remembers
how you took her back to the roller coaster's three
heart-racing minutes, a barely controlled panic
that never lets up after the first plunge.
I read her *National Enquirers*: "A True and False Guide
to Everything You Should Know about the Heart,"

"Expert Says Dreams Don't Mean a Thing." I suspect
the guide's more false, and that
there are no experts on memory's transformation
of landscape, or the recollection
of gone summers' amusements. I'm not sure
I have anything important to say
about memory or history, only how well
the park contains them: the beeping video game
settled beside the dusty mannequin
who promises the truth of love or fortune
as her mechanical hand moves back and forth
over a spread of cards meant to tell
what time might bring. Sentimental
as it sounds, nothing seems to touch
the carousel in the center of the park,
under its fretwork dome. The glass eyes
of the horses gleam, their new paint jobs
black and silver, orchid and rose –
legs thrown back, heads flung or tilted,
they rise and fall on their oiled poles
doubled by mirrors, turning under a ceiling
painted with garlands and moths, past little frescoes
of bathing beauties and exotic landscapes.
Perhaps it looks a little different now,
what with the chain-link fence,
maybe all the horses aren't the originals –
but anyone who ever spun in this circle
of rising and falling heard this same music,
or something like it, watched the tree

and rides blur, and saw behind them
this same parade of approaching horses –
tails high, saddles gleaming –
and before them the horses hurrying away.

The Pink Palace

My father would take me, Saturdays,
to an unfinished mansion: a rich eccentric
had built a few rooms and a facade
of pink granite before the money ran out
and the fragments became property of the state,
a museum for children. Of what
I'm not sure – I remember only one room,
a wall of tiny doors, some at floor level,
others all the way up to the ceiling.
I would open the lowest; he would hoist me
to others so I could stare inside until
he grew tired of holding me. Behind the doors,
behind glass, a tree, huge in memory,
hung with all the glory of taxidermy: robin
and jay, squirrels racing or paused, sitting upright,
everything that lived overhead.

Many windows: each would yield
a little. I thought if I could see it all
the tree would spread like a Sunday school story
of paradise, bearing up on its branches
all the finished houses of heaven. And these
were the citizens: openmouthed blackbird
fixed in the position of cry, eggs
arranged in the nest, incapable of change.
I know I magnified the tree.
Maybe if I'd seen it all at once
it could never have held so many –
the visible, the mostly hidden,

49

glowing feathers behind the leaves.
Were there leaves at all?

That summer the outings with my father ended.
The Pink Palace, and then nothing.
Whatever he intended, what he showed me
seemed a lesson – that no single view will hold.
As if he knew I'd need to tell myself
a story – one strong enough to carry me,
and not in his favor – and whatever I told myself
would be incomplete, that nothing will ever
be finished except the past, which is too large
to apprehend at once. All that changes
is the frame we choose. And so he said
as he clutched my waist between his two big hands, *See,
look at this one*, and held me higher.

Sideshow

The goat without ears coughs
softly. Canvas flaps ripple,
starred banners; this is the tent
of animals partial or possessed
of extra parts: the four-legged hen,
the ram sprouting a bouquet
of horns. The ewe drags a hooved bundle
on the dirty straw, and in a corner
the most troubling gaze,
a face that looks up as if
through a foot of lake water:
WORLD'S SMALLEST HORSE, B. 1976,
D. 1980. The paint on the rough sign
bleeds. And on the tent flap
someone painted him galloping,
shorter than daisies, on a meadow
impossibly green, mountains stunned
by rain. He never galloped;
the crooked little legs held him
a foot above the dirt he studied
day after day and now cannot
even enter. Cotton batting pushes
the iridescent glass eyes slightly askew,
his mouth sewn up into that crooked
but somehow forgiving smile, as if
even after suffering the lifetime
of a small horse it is all right
to remain on earth with his blind,
satisfied stare – lone star of squalor
in the miserable tent, my teacher.

Horses after a Hurricane

Hart Crane, Isle of Pines, 1926

How they eased out from the bamboo brake,
the morning the hurricane released us,
one ours and one unknown, jettisoned
on the creaking shore of what was left

of the veranda. But the whole *world*
was out of place that morning: bits
of the roof smithereened to Havana, stray
shack boards upended in the garden,
ragged oranges awash in the litter.
All night the housekeeper and her parrot –
sometimes you couldn't tell which cries
were hers and which Attaboy's shrieks –

hid under the biggest bed. And once
the thunder began to jab in that chain
of mountains across, I huddled under
with my sheaf of manuscript, evidence
that I'd felt that absolute music in the air
again, some tremendous rondure floating

somewhere – lurching out for *cervezas*
or to bring the Victrola nearer,
jazz all night while the plaster gave way,
striking chords on the untuned piano
as graceful as mine – I liked them better –
and once in the gray eye of the storm I rushed

out to the palm grove to piss and a sudden gust
took my shirt and trousers. "The picture of Adonis,"
Mrs. Simpson said, "striding through the tall grass
à la natural." In the morning,
we dragged the Victrola out on the veranda
and did a semi-Spanish one-step to "Valencia,"

soggy cushions balanced on our heads
and the woeful flotsam of the garden dripping
around us. And the town! What was never
too much in place now endlessly scattered:
grass licked black as patent leather,
a splayed mule tangled in the lot

like a Smith Corona thrown from an upstairs window,
and the upturned house of the idiot boy –
who'd smiled, rendingly beautiful, and danced
for laughing kids, shaking his big phallus
in the air, or talked to a blue little kite
high in the afternoon and examined cinders

through the telescope of a twice-opened
tomato can. He'd held onto the grass
all night when the privy where he and his mother
had hidden blew over and their suitcases
went whirling to Grand Cayman. Later
a letter from Alfredo, my Cuban sailor

of two bracing nights' acquaintance,
would read, *Maximo Gomez, my ship, him sink
in ciclon. All my clothes drowned.* The next day,
from a ship baking thousands of loaves
for our rescue, the most available sailors
came streaming onto the gale-shuffled docks,

all scalding white against the porpoise acres
from here to Havana. It was the Navy's grandest
picnic. So many disillusionments
are made bitter when faith is given
– with the sailor no faith is properly expected
and how jolly and cordial and warm

the touseling is sometimes, after all,
and a couple did shuck their uniforms on the floor
like heaps of white lilacs. But I was talking
horses – that white one came out of nowhere
and stood with old Don, our dray, snuffled
at the weather in his nose, at the end

of it, awash in the aura of that remembered
night, the best of my life, and Mrs. Simpson
and I named him, laughing, and I saw him
even while I talked Bacardi and USA in Mack's
with the gobs, and after, when we were faithless,
and entirely tender.

Shaker Orchard

Holding even flowers subject
to the principle of use,
the Shakers invented

the notion of packaged seeds
and a steam-powered
distiller for rose water.

They uncluttered rooms
till space filled
with Universal Light –

white walls, a chest, a chair
hung on pegs beside a broom
so perfect in its simplicity

as to become a pure channel:
there was nothing in those lines
to impede the flow

of the divine, no ornament
to distract the mind from Love.
Work, Ann Lee said, as though

you had a thousand years to live;
thus the tiny stitches
in a sister's cotton cap, the exact lid

of a pine box. Pestered
by holy doves delivering
gifts – exotic telegrams of fruit,

flower and verse – Mother Ann danced
to come to terms with the demands
of angels. In one print

the brothers and sisters
in their separate portions of the room
thunder on the polished floorboards.

They swept clean. Clear
the excess, they knew,
and light will pour in

as in certain American landscapes
where light itself occupies space,
whole regions of luminosity.

Seeing the turn of things
and unwilling to propagate,
they were swept away.

The last,
four elderly sisters,
live at Sabbathday Lake;

the brothers are twenty years gone.
In October their grapes yield,
suspended from the arbor

as if to recall a paradise of ease
where we had only to look upward
to be fed, and the apple trees

hold out their thousands of small victories,
having managed both to contain light
and to bear.

For Louise Michel

Above all else, I am taken
by the Revolution.

You wished
dogs would bite
the men beating them,
horses throw their harsh riders,

watched "peasants cut frogs
in two, keeping the rear legs to fry,
leaving the front part
to creep away, seek
to bury itself
in mud."

And geese: "their webbed feet
nailed to the floor
to keep them from moving
while they're fattened
for slaughter."

Later, in your cell at Clermont,
a mouse you'd fed
began to leave
bits of crust and droppings
beneath your pillow,
so that you, touched, wrote in your *Memóires*
"Bread for all!"

* * *

You trade spools, scrawls of pearl cotton
for linnet nests,
read from the thick, illustrated history of Rome.

The wind stumbles through the unglazed windows
of your father's house.
Your mother continues
to work in the kitchen,
to work as everyone must.

Clatter of crochet hooks, needles,
a thin shawl of snow
over the windows of the *écrègne*:
loose petals, feathers from a shook pillow.

* * *

"Once near our château on the hill down which vine-
yards sloped, men with clubs had surrounded a poor she-
wolf that howled, her offspring in her arms. I begged
mercy for her, but naturally it wasn't granted. . . . The
mercy that as a child I asked for her I wouldn't ask now for
the men who behave worse than wolves."

* * *

There is a spark in each petal of the magnolia
and if we cradle it we might be changed,

as the choir of frogs is changed
when its antiphonal flies into the summer
wind toward darkness,

changed like the white goose with blood-spattered feathers,
the parricide led to the guillotine
in a village near yours,
changed like the horse
in the medical academy at Alfort
trembling on legs
where its hooves were once,

but no longer believing the credo of the women
in the snowy silence and sighing
of the *écrègne*:
"Everybody can't eat bread every day."

* * *

Your hand slips
behind this page,
shadow behind the parchment shade
of a lamp.

You conclude your memoirs:
"Do they still send soldiers
against the people?"

Hair

In a scene in the film
shot at Bergen–Belsen days after
the liberation of the camp
a woman brushes her hair.

Though her gesture is effortless
it seems also for the first time,
as if she has just remembered
that she has long hair,

that it is a pleasure
to brush, and that pleasure
is possible. And the mirror
beside which the camera must be rolling,

the combing out and tying back
of the hair, all possible.
She wears a new black sweater
the relief workers have brought,

clothes to replace the body's
visible hungers. Perhaps
she is a little shy of the camera,
or else she is distracted

by the new wool and plain wonder
of the hairbrush, because
on her face is a sort of dulled,
dreamy look, as if the part

63

of herself that recognizes
the simple familiar good of brushing
is floating back into her,
the way the spiritualists say

the etheric body returns to us
when we wake from sleep's long travel.
With each stroke she restores
something of herself, and one

at a time the arms and hands
and face remember, the scalp
remembers that her hair
is a part of her, her own.

To Cavafy

We were talking about desire,
how sometimes only an image,
a surface compells us:
that boy, for instance, we watched
from the shore, standing with his back
half-turned to us out on the little raft

on Pond Number 10. Five divers –
characters in a story
I am inventing as much as remembering –
had paused on the raft,
in the air beginning to haze,
five o'clock light, the end

of August. Though they are only
a few feet apart, the distance
between them is carefully kept;
two study the water,
one looks away to the bank's
vague border. On the left,

the tallest are standing, high-school boys:
one faces toward us, arms
folded across his chest, taciturn,
shadowed, but light catches
his splendid friend's
wet shoulders and makes of them

a white bar in the misting afternoon.
It is almost too late to be swimming.
The gleaming one stands so surely,
legs spread just enough apart,
perhaps rocking back and forth a little.
What was only a remembered surface –

light on a boy's shoulders –
acquires depth, becomes nearly three-dimensional
as it is reconstructed;
I can sense, if not quite see,
the pond water streaming down
his shoulders. Is it solipsism

to love not the world
but what you make of it?
Or is that what we mean when we say
"memorable" – that we take something
from the surface of things and make it
ours? For him I might imagine

any present, any history, but what I see
are the loose green trunks he wears,
ones he's probably had for years,
he wears them so effortlessly.
The green water whitens his skin.
I think now his chest and arms

are becoming a little cool.
He and his companion are talking
and not talking, a low, laconic conversation,
without substance. As he is now,
really, since he is a memory reinvented,
and in the way of the stories we make

for ourselves out of whatever strikes us,
whatever makes us need stories,
something should happen. Nothing did;
he never knew we were watching.
I swam to the raft, waved to you
on the shore, slipped back into the water.

Of course we wanted him,
but more than that – we have
each other's bodies, better
because they are familiar.
We wanted to enter the way
he dove unselfconsciously

from the little dock,
certain; the diver
becomes pure form, the exact shape
for parting water. I think had there
been a single question in his head
he would have disappeared,

or have been someone else,
and I think, imagining him,
of Cavafy, of encounters in upstairs rooms
recollected in upstairs rooms.
His must have been a life upstairs,
remembering what happened over there,

beside the washstand, where the blind
would edit half the bed
with its dark crosshatching.
Someone he met on a streetcar,
over a counter of handkerchiefs,
someone he could remember.

For a little while their caps
would hang on a hook beside the door,
those men so fleeting in body –
a train to catch, an appointment –
becoming more mute and ideal,
more permanent as they were revised.

Had his hand passed right through them –
the iris-blue vein in a chiseled arm,
a thick, dusky wrist – I don't know
that it would have mattered. I don't know
that he ever really wanted to touch anyone.

Charlie Howard's Descent

Between the bridge and the river
he falls through
a huge portion of night;
it is not as if falling

is something new. Over and over
he slipped into the gulf
between what he knew and how
he was known. What others wanted

opened like an abyss: the laughing
stock-clerks at the grocery, women
at the luncheonette amused by his gestures.
What could he do, live

with one hand tied
behind his back? So he began to fall
into the star-faced section
of night between the trestle

and the water because he could not meet
a little town's demands,
and his earrings shone and his wrists
were as limp as they were.

I imagine he took the insults in
and made of them a place to live;
we learn to use the names
because they are there,

familiar furniture: *faggot*
was the bed he slept in, hard
and white, but simple somehow,
queer something sharp

but finally useful, a tool,
all the jokes a chair,
stiff-backed to keep the spine straight,
a table, a lamp. And because

he's fallen for twenty-three years,
despite whatever awkwardness
his flailing arms and legs assume
he is beautiful

and like any good diver
has only an edge of fear
he transforms into grace.
Or else he is not afraid,

and in this way climbs back
up the ladder of his fall,
out of the river into the arms
of the three teenage boys

who hurled him from the edge –
really boys now, afraid,
their fathers' cars shivering behind them,
headlights on – and tells them

it's all right, that he knows
they didn't believe him
when he said he couldn't swim,
and blesses his killers

in the way that only the dead
can afford to forgive.

Independence Day

Benches spangled in shade,
billows of bunting in river breeze,
the esplanade blazing: blanket to blanket
and cooler to cooler, their quarter-million radios'
zones of sound overlapping, a quarter-million
have gathered early for the fireworks.

The two of us can't help but feel part
of this immense party: everywhere
we are spread on quilts, masked in visors
and sunglasses. The collective future's decided,
I guess, by these crowds – more of us
than I'll ever see in one place, and all out

for a good time. We all stake claims:
sometimes even a makeshift tent or string fence
marks a chosen portion of view,
though everyone seems more interested
in the community of viewers. We wonder
if the scene might be much different in war

or disaster – these could be refugees
lugging their portable households –
but these are cheerful explosions, surprises
and mock danger everyone seems to like.
Glow-in-the-dark headbands begin to shine
as evening comes on, electric pink

or blue, as if the buyer could wear a thin stripe
of the neon that will later burst
over the water, a fire to keep.
The faces of the vendors
who carry hundreds in swaying bundles
glow in the light of their fifty-cent toys.

Threading through the crowd's a man
we almost know – Don, a street character
we always try to avoid because he'll regale us forever
with the same old stories – the kind
whose tone makes you feel you are included in his past
more than you've allowed him into yours,

that everything you've ever said to him was cherished.
One can see why: the evidence
of twenty years' drinking tattoos his face.
We'd see him and his lover on street corners
Saturday nights – Don loud and boozing,
talking to anyone he thought he recognized –

of course not hearing anything they said –
so like a porcupine in his lurching walk
one would expect him to snuffle and root for food.
Silent Andy, lean and pale, always in black
to match his hair dye, a thin confused smile
suggesting that while he understood nothing

of what was happening around him
that was not such a bad thing. Always Don had
recollection – "Remember when I did that big drag
and I sang right to you and you loved it" –
and news: once the building beside theirs burned,
sparks and old bricks tumbling into the street

beside the ruins of the fire escape. In his condition
Don couldn't carry much, but I believed him
when he said he lugged Andy out of the smoke,
a sluggish weight, though from the look of him
anyone could carry that slight frame
narrowed by whiskey.

I imagined him on Don's back, stubble face
lying against his lover's shoulder, thin legs
and black boots dangling. They were sizes
too big – stuffed, maybe, with newspapers
or handkerchiefs to make him taller.
Tonight the story's different:

"You won't be seeing Andy anymore. I woke up
and found him dead two nights ago. . ." Then
the story's all a tumble: how a swollen leg
led to a burst heart. How Don won't move
but keep their place the same, sixteen years,
not enough, how he's come here because

they would have. How his friends collected forty dollars
for the funeral, something quiet, on Saturday;
how trying to keep the daily patterns
Don sat down at eleven o'clock alone
and said without thinking, "Honey,
do you want a glass of soda

while we watch the 'Twilight Zone'?"
It's that evidence of habit that moves most –
the way any of us would turn to touch
a familiar arm, the way a familiar chair
supports us when we expect it to
and does not disappear. As fireworks do,

those spider chrysanthemums
of our collective independence. They're the wonders
of July: spark fountains,
bright arcs over the shadowy bulk
of boats clustered on the wharf.
Each is greeted by a sigh of recognition

that seems to say, *There it is.* That *oh*
declares our mutual acceptance of the flares,
the will to say to one another *Yes,*
I see it too, even as the sky burns.
And the bright fragments twirl and chatter down
as if even the stars spoke to each other as they fell.

Bethlehem in Broad Daylight

For my mother and father

Harbor Lights

I'm coming home through the red lacquered lobby,
    corridors the bitter green of gingko
        marred by the transoms' milky light.

I am sixteen and the room's three-fifty a night
    in the Chinese hotel on Water Street,
        and I've been out again to the grocery

where they sell cigarettes, one for a dime,
    and to look at the stone face
        in the shop window. I'm calling her

the angel, the mother of angels, and chiseled
    upon the marble of her face is a veil
        so thin it isn't stone at all

but something that emerges out of her chill dreaming.
    It's like watching your mother sleep,
        minutes after you have been conceived,

and her closed eyes say it's all right
    to wake alone, almost at evening, in a city hotel
        where all night from the room next door

comes the sound, I swear, of chopping.
    It's the room of the old woman
        the men at the desk call Mama, and the best

I can imagine is that she's working late
     for the cafe down the block,
          cleaving celery, splitting the white

and acid green of bok choi. All day
     she'll wash the floors in the halls,
          hissing to herself in sounds I imagine

are curses, damning the residue of the streets
     the residents track all night
          onto the speckled constellations

of the linoleum. She scrubs until it's flawless
     as black water off the piers down the block,
          until the floors gleam green under the window

where RESIDENTIAL shimmers, watery electric
     shantung blossoming over and over
          two stories above the street.

Nights like this, when it's raining
     and the chill seems almost visible,
          coming in across the Sound and the waterfront's

rambling warehouses, the radiator pronounces,
     almost exactly, my mother's name.
          Then the pipes with their silver garlands

sing *runaway*. I've taken the pill I bought
　　on the corner, where someone's always reciting
　　　　the litany of an impossible future:

Purple Doubledome, Blue Microdot, Sunshine.
　　I'm waiting for the flowers in the cracked linoleum
　　　　to twist and open, scrubbed into blossom,

waiting for the harbor lights
　　to burn – the night caught in my hotel window
　　　　like a piece of film in a projector,

melting, so that light comes searing out of the darkness
　　first as boiling pinpricks, then a whole angel.
　　　　What I've bought is nothing, aspirin

or sugar, but I don't know that,
　　and I'm waiting to come on. It's raining harder,
　　　　the knife in the next room striking

the block, the glass beading up
　　and then erasing itself, shimmering the lights,
　　　　and the stone face around the corner

dreams her way out of the world
　　of appearances behind her window,
　　　　her glaze of rain, her veil.

Anna Karenina

This morning a hurrying white boat
ripped between the plum tree
and the harbor's rippling sateen;
by afternoon whitecaps break

far out from shore, and gulls reel
by this off-season rental, angels on wires
in a lavish pageant of storm.
Wild grapes scour the roof,

a stunted trunk scrapes
the wet black siding; the wind
investigates anything, like someone
picking through a rummage table

in a terrible hurry. For days
I've grown used to silence;
yesterday I didn't see anyone
but the woman who trundles

every morning toward the canal,
her kerchief flapping blue wings,
her constitutional a bitter duty.
Now the whole house leans

into the wind as she did, and my smoldering fire
and waterjug of sea lavender
seem futile gestures to warm
this summer house pinned to a dune

held by grass and a ribbon of wooden wall.
All day I've been reading *Anna Karenina*,
returning to the chapter in which Tolstoy
brings Anna back to the house in Petersburg,

after the bitter separation, the dawning
awareness that her new lover will not perfect her
after all, when she stands by the bedside
of her son. The boy curls and blinks

out of the deep water of a child's sleep,
lifts himself and then falls,
not back to the pillow, but
into her arms. They had told him

she was dead, but he never believed them,
and though he's falling back
into dream even as he speaks,
he says, "Today is my birthday,

I knew you'd come." Because
she has never stopped longing
for him, she has not imagined
he has grown. And because

the boy can't say what he knows –
that she is perfect and unhappy –
he tells her how he fell on a hill
in the park, and somersaulted three times,

and she forgets to open the bag of toys
she chose the day before. It's dusk,
the storm hardly let up,
but the little triangle of sail

skitters over the water again,
milky gray as the moths that fold
against the windows. How do they hold on?
I can't imagine how cold the sailor

must be, though I can guess
something of his exhilaration –
how the sail must fill and push
against him. I think I might see

the woman in blue making her way
down the shore again, only
to feel that pressure. And the mother
who's lost everything sits on the edge

of the coverlets with such tenderness,
the weight of her son against her, though
she is barely able to be with him at all,
her thoughts are on the future so.

The Ancient World

Today the Masons are auctioning
their discarded pomp: a trunk of turbans,
gemmed and ostrich-plumed, and operetta costumes
labeled inside the collar "Potentate"
and "Vizier." Here their chairs, blazoned
with the Masons' sign, huddled
like convalescents, lean against one another

on the grass. In a casket are rhinestoned poles
the hierophants carried in parades;
here's a splendid golden staff some ranking officer waved,
topped with a golden pyramid and a tiny,
inquisitive sphinx. No one's worn this stuff
for years, and it doesn't seem worth buying;
where would we put it? Still,

I want that staff. I used to love
to go to the library – the smalltown brick refuge
of those with nothing to do, really,
"Carnegie" chiseled on the pediment
above columns that dwarfed an inconsequential street.
Embarrassed to carry the same book past
the water fountain's plaster centaurs

up to the desk again, I'd take
The Wonders of the World to the Reading Room
where Art and Industry met in the mural
on the dome. The room smelled like two decades
before I was born, when the name

carved over the door meant something.
I never read the second section,

"Wonders of the Modern World";
I loved the promise of my father's blueprints,
the unfulfilled turquoise schemes,
but in the real structures
you could hardly imagine a future.
I wanted the density of history,
which I confused with the smell of the book:

Babylon's ziggurat tropical with ferns,
engraved watercourses rippling;
the Colossus of Rhodes balanced
over the harbormouth on his immense ankles.
Athena filled one end of the Parthenon,
in an "artist's reconstruction,"
like an adult in a dollhouse.

At Halicarnassus, Mausolus remembered himself
immensely, though in the book
there wasn't even a sketch,
only a picture of huge fragments.
In the pyramid's deep clockworks,
did the narrow tunnels mount toward
the eye of God? That was the year

photos were beamed back from space;
falling asleep I used to repeat a new word

to myself, *telemetry*, liking the way
it seemed to allude to something storied.
The earth was whorled marble,
at that distance. Even the stuck-on porticoes
and collonades downtown were narrative,

somehow, but the buildings my father engineered
were without stories. All I wanted
was something larger than our ordinary sadness –
greater not in scale but in context,
memorable, true to a proportioned,
subtle form. Last year I knew a student,
a half mad boy who finally opened his arms

with a razor, not because he wanted to die
but because he wanted to design something grand
on his own body. Once he said, *When a child
realizes his parents aren't enough,
he turns to architecture.*
I think I know what he meant.
Imagine the Masons parading,

one of them, in his splendid get-up,
striding forward with the golden staff,
above his head Cheops' beautiful shape –
a form we cannot separate
from the stories about the form,
even if we hardly know them,
even if it no longer signifies, if it only shines.

A Collection of Minerals

Weekdays on the island my father
engineered a road past the pink
and blue of empty summer houses
to the missile silo; he took me down once
into the corrugated metal shaft

where the white rocket would be
lowered into place, covered over
with brush and earth once the warhead
was assembled. That afternoon
I reeled in a yellowtail,

a disk of a fish
the color of his bulldozers,
gills fluttering on the narrow body
only my thumb's width from eye
to windshield eye: glittering

fool's gold, no good
to eat. Then, my father intent
on the water, my line rushed in zigzags
like a faultline opening;
what I pulled onto the metal pier

was a rainbowed thrust
of slick muscle coiling
far from anything it knew,
shuddering in air as if
it were in pain, as if

it required secrecy
and darkness. My father ran
to the back of his flatbed
– the government truck, its number
stenciled in a chalky tattoo –

rifled in his toolbox for the machete
he oiled and sharpened Saturday mornings.
This was Titusville, Florida,
the year our class practiced
climbing under our desks,

holding our hands over our faces
and eyes; our mothers stocked up
on canned goods, making caches
beneath the kitchen sink, "in case,"
and men bought knifes or rifles

for "protection." How sad we must have looked,
the fourth grade kneeling
on the marbled linoleum
while our teacher described the sirens,
what would become of the windows,

and offered us the defense
of our formica desktops placed squarely
between ourselves and unimaginable
light. In my mineral collection,
a box of little stones glued in rows

and labeled – feldspar, amethyst,
pyrite – there was a tiny green chunk
of uranium. I'd opened the box
in the dark to see if it would glow
like the face of my parents' alarm,

expecting its chilly radiance
to steal over my bed as it burned out
its half-life. But nothing happened,
and so I kept it in a drawer,
thinking it would change something,

something it touched might become important
or gigantic. When the teacher said
if the bomb fell our bodies would change,
I thought of the jagged surface
of the stone, ancient

and at home in the dark. My father
hacked at the eel until
there were only fragments
of the rippling it had been;
even the pieces

twisted on the steel pier
until he swept them over the edge
with the blade, and told me to pack
my tackle box, and drove me home –
where I was restless, and felt

something had been violated, cut apart
from its submerged privacy,
and the stones in the case seemed puny
and trivial, the sheen of the satin spar
unlikely and disturbing, the uranium

turned inward, revealing nothing,
and in a while I tore the stones loose
from the box one by one and traded them
for something I now cannot remember.

The Garden of the Moon

The school bus rattled around more turns
in the desert roads than I'd ever
be able to trace again, the summer I worked
in Head Start and the lead teacher
arranged a field trip from the barrio
to the Valley of the Moon.

We parked at a high ramshackle fence
straddling a swatch of creosote and mesquite.
There was nothing to the old man
swinging open the gate but shape –
black clothes, black beekeeper's hat –
and as his glove smoothed the veil

he welcomed us, in a sort of stage whisper,
to the Valley of the Moon, *built with the love*
and spiritual assistance of many,
and he led us in. The children walked with partners,
the teacher watching for stragglers or hazard;
I was assigned to Antonio, the boy

she mistrusted most. The path climbed
to shoulder-high alps of cement encrusted
with broken crockery and bits of glass,
junk mosaics capped with figures:
a chipped chalk-ware Snow White gathered
her glittered skirt, looking forward eagerly

from her high-collared cape as if everything
were about to be delivered to her.
At the mouth of a little cave the children
were instructed to dig for treasure;
they kicked till they found pennies in the sand,
and the teacher asked if they were meant to keep them.

The old man told us to speak softly,
if at all, because we were coming
to a place of great serenity,
and he led us down a curving stair
into a two-story grotto he'd hollowed
out of earth; weathered concrete seats

ringed a washtub pool, a mynah bird whispered
in a metal cage. *Whenever you are troubled,*
the old man said, *send your thoughts here.*
The bird spoke a few phrases for us;
even Antonio concentrated on its black sheen,
the old man's gestures. Water dripped

along one wall and I noticed how small
his battered black shoes were
on the ground he'd made himself.
Everywhere around the rim of this one were other,
unfinished gardens, a world of things
he might use to build them. *Your astral body*

can travel to the Garden of the Moon.
Later, in a leaning circus tent filled
with empty cages and Victorian photographs
of fairies, he performed a little lame magic,
which the children liked best,
along with the pennies: bouquets

pulled from sleeves, a dove
from a jiggling hat. The air
would never lift the veil enough
to show his face. At the gate
he'd hand us each a business card
stitched with a scarlet sequin,

printed with the motto, The Key
to the Fairy Treasure House Up,
Up in the Valley of the Moon,
and we'd file onto the bus where
the driver waited, reading a magazine,
and flash our brilliant souvenirs

in the windows all the way home.
But in the magic tent, when a real snake
emerged from a basket and a winged glimmer
slid down a wire and landed in a bloom
of smoke and sparks, Antonio forgot himself
enough to hold my hand, and leaned forward

like the statuette of Snow White,
with that same breathless look.

Isis: Dorothy Eady, 1924

I was never this beautiful.
I don't know if anyone can see how much more
I've become tonight, when the boys
    hired to play Nubians still the peacock fans,
        and another girl and I,

    in simple white robes tied with golden sashes,
perform "The Lament of Isis and Nephthys,"
in the Andrew Long translation:
    Sing we Osiris dead, soft on the dead
        that liveth are we calling.

The scene represents dawn,
and before the painted canvas riverbank
we are kneeling over the void
    left by my husband the God.
        Dorothy, my friend said,

    how should I pose? I told her
to bend as though we were mourning
the world's first grief, though of course
    there is no body, since God
        has been torn to pieces

    and I am to spend an eon
reassembling him. In the floodlamps
she speaks the text in her best elocution,
    fixed in a tragic tableau,
        and she makes no mistakes,

though she brushes the fringe
of the dropcloth once and for an instant
Egypt ripples. And though this pageant
    on the stage of my father's theatre
        isn't any more than prelude

to the cinema, I live my role,
the world I remember – I *do* remember –
restored to an uncompromised luster,
    not a single figure defaced
        on the wall of anyone's tomb.

He *was* my husband,
and I know he had to break apart,
in the ancient world, and tonight,
    so that in thousands of years,
        in the intimacy of dreams,

the pageant's trance,
I could reconstruct him
bit by bit, like so many shards.
    Anything can be restored,
        even his golden hands.

There is no time here,
where I am, on the stage of the Plymouth Theatre,
reciting the lament the people used to walk
    from Thebes to Abydos to hear,
        rendered into English verse wrongly,

though the audience accepts it,
as they always have, and are moved.

Ararat

Wrapped in gold foil, in the search
and shouting of Easter Sunday,
it was the ball of the princess,
it was Pharoah's body
sleeping in its golden case.
At the foot of the picket fence,
in grass lank with the morning rain,
it was a Sunday school prize,
silver for second place, gold
for the triumphant little dome
of Ararat, and my sister
took me by the hand and led me
out onto the wide, wet lawn
and showed me to bend into the thick nests
of grass, into the darkest green.
Later I had to give it back,
in exchange for a prize,
though I would rather have kept the egg.
What might have coiled inside it?
Crocuses tight on their clock-springs,
a bird who'd sing himself into an angel
in the highest reaches of the garden,
the morning's flaming arrow?
Any small thing can save you.
Because the golden egg gleamed
in my basket once, though my childhood
became an immense sheet of darkening water
I was Noah, and I was his ark,
and there were two of every animal inside me.

Beginners

The year Miss Tynes enrolled our class
in the Object of the Month Club,
a heavy box arrived each month
from the Metropolitan Museum.
What emerged once – when volunteers

opened each latch, and one lucky girl
lifted the wooden lid away –
was an Egyptian cat, upright on its haunches,
unapproachable, one golden earring flashing,
a carved cartouche between its legs.
Miss Tynes read a translation of the hieroglyphics
and a paragraph depicting the glory

of thousands of mummies ranged on shelves
in the dark – cased and muslined cats,
ibis, baboons – their jewelry ready to offer
any sliver of sunlight back, if it ever touched them.
Later, the cat ruled the back of the room,
fixed on a countertop beside a model

of the planets and a display of moths.
When we'd finished our work it was all right
to go and stand beside it,
even, if we were careful, touch it.
I'd read a story in which two children
drank an emerald medicine from a pharmacy urn

forgot their parents, and understood
the speech of cats. Their adventures were nocturnal
and heroic, and their cat became, I think,
the King of Cats, and was lost to them,
so they drank red medicine from the drugstore urn,
and returned to the human world

of speech. I cried, not for their lost pet
but for the loss of language, and my father
forbade me sad books. Some days, after school,
I'd go to my friend Walter's, and we'd play
a simple game: because he was smaller than me,
though no younger, Walter would be the son.

He'd take off his shirt and sit in my lap;
I'd put my arms around him
and rub his stomach, and he would pretend
to cry or be content, liking my hands.
We were ten, or eight. It's too easy
to think of our game as sex before we knew

what bodies could do, before bodies could do
much. There was something else,
at least for me: the pleasure
of touching what became pure form,
not Walter anymore but the sensation
of skin over supple muscle. I was the heroic

father, I loved – not him, exactly,
with his narrow crewcut head which reminded me,
even then, of a mouse – but the formal thing
he'd become, in his room, with the door closed.
We never changed roles; I was the good lover,
I fathered him. We knew enough to keep

the game private, less out of guilt
than a sense of something exposure
might dilute. It was like the way the children
in my class touched the cat, even talked to it,
hesitantly, beginners in a new language,
maybe imagined it might speak back to us.

Though it was the perfect confidant,
since it could take in anything
and remain calm and black and golden
until it was packed away in the varnished box
to another school, where other children
might lean toward it and whisper,
until it was more ancient, with all it knew.

63rd Street Y

All night steam heat pours
from radiators and up the stairwells
to the thirteenth floor,
and I can't sleep because I know
all the windows are thrown wide open,

a voyeur's advent calendar.
If I lean out the screenless frame
the building's twin flanks yield
banks of lit rectangles above a black courtyard
where a few papers lie completely still,

this warm December. Thirteen dizzying stories
show tonight and any night some blank shades
or black glass, and dozens of interiors –
men all right, mostly not young
or strikingly Christian, though certainly associated.

The nude black man two windows over
is lying in bed, Melchior halfway
through his journey, writing a letter home.
And on the twelfth floor, in my favorite window,
only a little corner holding

the foot of the bed visible,
a pair of strong arms are smoothing
a thin red coverlet so carefully
he must be expecting someone. The scene's
too fragmentary to construct a convincing story,

but he smooths the cloth until
I imagine there's not a single wrinkle
on the scarlet spread blushing
the lamplight so that his arms glow
with the color of intimacy. Even

after I'm tired of watching
there's something all night to wake me:
a pigeon flapping toward the sill
like an awkward annunciation, someone singing
in the alley thirteen floors down

– the Ode to Joy? – curiosity
about the red room a floor below, empty now.
In the park, the lamps' circles shrink
along distant paths beneath intricate trees,
Fifth Avenue luminous in its Roman,

floodlit splendor, and there the hulk
of the Metropolitan, where the Neapolitan angels
must be suspended in darkness now,
their glazed silks dim,
though their tempera skin's so polished

even an exit sign would set them blazing.
I'm sleeping a little then thinking
of the single male angel, lithe and radiant,
wrapped only in a Baroque scrap
sculpted by impossible wind. Because

he's slightly built – real, somehow –
there's something shocking
in his nakedness, the svelte hips
barely brushed by drapery;
he's no sexless bearer of God's thoughts.

Divinity includes desire
– why else create a world
like this one, dawn fogging
the park in gold, the Moorish arches
of the Y one grand Italian Bethlehem

in which the minor figures wake
in anticipation of some unforeseen beginning.
Even the pigeons seem glazed
and expectant, fired to iridescence.
And on the twelfth floor

just the perfect feet and ankles
of the boy in the red-flushed room
are visible. I think he must be disappointed,
stirring a little, alone, and then
two other legs enter the rectangle of view,

moving toward his and twining with them,
one instep bending to stroke
the other's calf. They make me happy,
these four limbs in effortless conversation
on their snowy ground, the sheets

curling into the billows sculptors used once
to make the suspension of gravity
visible. It doesn't matter
that it isn't silk. I haven't much evidence
to construe what binds them,

but the narrative windows
will offer all morning the glad tidings
of union, comfort and joy,
though I will not stay to watch them.

The Death of Antinoüs

When the beautiful young man drowned –
accidentally, swimming at dawn
in a current too swift for him,
or obedient to some cult
of total immersion that promised
the bather would come up divine,

mortality rinsed from him –
Hadrian placed his image everywhere,
a marble Antinoüs staring across
the public squares where a few dogs
always scuffled, planted
in every squalid little crossroad

at the farthest corners of the Empire.
What do we want in any body
but the world? And if the lover's
inimitable form was nowhere,
then he would find it everywhere,
though the boy became simply more dead

as the sculptors embodied him.
Wherever Hadrian might travel,
the beloved figure would be there
first: the turn of his shoulders,
the exact marble nipples,
the drowned face not really lost

to the Nile – which has no appetite,
merely takes in anything
without judgment or expectation –
but lost into its own multiplication,
an artifice rubbed with oils and acid
so that the skin might shine.

Which of these did I love?
Here is his hair, here his hair
again. Here the chiseled liquid waist
I hold because I cannot hold it.
If only one of you, he might have said
to any of the thousand marble boys anywhere,

would speak. Or the statues might have been enough,
the drowned boy blurred as much by memory
as by water, molded toward an essential,
remote ideal. Longing, of course,
becomes its own object, the way
that desire can make anything into a god.

Tiara

Peter died in a paper tiara
cut from a book of princess paper dolls;
he loved royalty, sashes

and jewels. *I don't know,*
he said, when he woke in the hospice,
I was watching the Bette Davis film festival

on Channel 57 and then —
At the wake, the tension broke
when someone guessed

the casket closed because
he was *in there in a big wig
and heels,* and someone said,

*You know he's always late,
he probably isn't here yet —
he's still fixing his makeup.*

And someone said he asked for it.
Asked for it —
when all he did was go down

into the salt tide
of wanting as much as he wanted,
giving himself over so drunk

or stoned it almost didn't matter who,
though they were beautiful,
stampeding into him in the simple,

ravishing music of their hurry.
I think heaven is perfect stasis
poised over the realms of desire,

where dreaming and waking men lie
on the grass while wet horses
roam among them, huge fragments

of the music we die into
in the body's paradise.
Sometimes we wake not knowing

how we came to lie here,
or who has crowned us with these temporary,
precious stones. And given

the world's perfectly turned shoulders,
the deep hollows blued by longing,
given the irreplaceable silk

of horses rippling in orchards,
fruit thundering and chiming down,
given the ordinary marvels of form

and gravity, what could he do,
what could any of us ever do
but ask for it?

Playland

The piano player's straightened hair
gleams wet under a blue spot, and he strikes
up an arpeggio, and everyone up the long
steep stairs at the Playland Café sings:
Pack up all my cares and woes . . .
It is not a café, but a sort of sequin

buried in the smoked skin of a neighborhood
of old leather and garment lofts, soot-stained facades,
the lower floors spangled with peep shows
and arcades, and the neon blinks above the black entry
to the black and raspberry moiré room
where the drag queen behind the piano and a cocktail

gestures the lyrics *No one here can love
or understand me* with one hand,
as if reaching to gather in her audience.
They can, certainly do, and she draws her hand
back toward herself effortlessly, as if
through long habit it no longer requires

even her attention. The black bar, the empty stage
with its tinsel curtains don't ever change,
though the place is spangled for every holiday,
probably nearly single-handedly
keeping the crepe-paper-streamer industry alive –
and tonight it's decked for the Fourth of July,

Miss Liberty's birthday, and the jokes are sweet
and inevitable: Who's carrying the torch,
who's under those skirts, whose legs
are spread in the harbor? The drunk
who wants to bless and marry us
makes the sign of the cross and rambles

in Latin, and though it's silly
it makes me want to stay here all night.
I've never seen anyone but us leave,
and I believe that everyone here
has been dead for years,
and that they not only don't mind

but are truly happy, because here
there is no need to guard themselves,
no possibility of an aesthetic mistake,
and no one is too old, too poor
or mistaken. When the queen walks by
in her black pumps – she must have tried heels

and given up, though somehow her walk
still creates the impression of heels –
she walks for all of us: aerial,
haughty, not bothering to look to either side,
intent on what she's made of herself
and how, and where she's going

– which is only the bar,
draped with bunting, but she might as well
be walking to her own country. Which is this one:
undeniably dangerous and slated,
probably, for demolition, but forgiving;
anyone's taken in, liberties given

to all comers here at the bottom,
where no one wills to come. *Oh,*
everyone does, but would you go home
with anyone here? Besides,
it's early yet. Forgiveness
for her tired hair – her own,

for the black dress accentuating her wide shoulders,
the same rhinestones. It doesn't matter;
another night of artifice is as exhausting
as it is necessary. I hope
she walks forever: that the sign
over the black door keeps pronouncing

its credo, *Playland,* that the piano player,
his voice embalmed in gravel and honey
continues, *Yes, light the light, I'll be home*
late tonight.

Adonis Theater

It must have seemed the apex of dreams,
the movie palace on Eighth Avenue
with its tiered chrome ticket-booth,
Tibetan, the phantom blonde head

of the cashier floating
in its moon window. They'd outdone each other
all over the neighborhood, raising
these blunt pastiches of anywhere

we couldn't go: a pagoda, a future,
a Nepal. The avenue fed into the entry
with its glass cases of radiant stars,
their eyes dreamy and blown

just beyond human proportions to prepare us
for how enormous they would become inside,
after the fantastic ballroom of the lobby,
when the uniformed usher would show the way

to seats reserved for us in heaven.
I don't know when it closed,
or if it ever shut down entirely,
but sometime – the forties? –

they stopped repainting the frescoes,
and when the plaster fell they merely
swept it away, and allowed
the gaps in the garlands of fruit

that decked the ceiling above the second balcony.
The screen shrunk to a soiled blank
where these smaller films began to unreel,
glorifying not the face but the body.

Or rather, bodies, ecstatic
and undifferentiated as one film ends
and the next begins its brief and awkward exposition
before it reaches the essential

matter of flesh. No one pays much attention
to the screen. The viewers wander
in the steady, generous light washing back
up the long aisles toward the booth.

Perhaps we're hurt by becoming
beautiful in the dark, whether we watch
Douglas Fairbanks escaping from a dreamed,
suavely oriental city – think of those leaps

from the parapet, how he almost flies
from the grasp of whatever would limit him –
or the banal athletics of two or more men who were
and probably remain strangers. Perhaps

there's something cruel in the design
of the exquisite plaster box
built to frame the exotic
and call it desirable. When the show's over,

it is, whether it's the last frame
of Baghdad or the impossibly extended
come shot. And the solitary viewers,
the voyeurs and married men go home,

released from the swinging chrome doors
with their splendid reliefs
of the implements of artistry,
released into the streets as though washed

in something, marked with some temporary tatoo
that will wear away on the train ride home,
before anyone has time to punish them for it.
Something passing, even though the blood,

momentarily, has broken into flower
in the palace of limitless desire –
how could one ever be *done* with a god?
All its illusion conspires,

as it always has, to show us one another
in this light, whether we look to
or away from the screen.

A Row of Identical Cottages

All night the flag outside our window
rippled above wet lilacs and someone's motorbike
        parked on the guest-house lawn.

At dawn I watched the houses lean
and crowd toward the pier, picket fences tumbling,
        the roses akimbo. Then the cycle

stuttered, the flag flapped
like a towel hung out to dry
        – starry field fading – and the sheet

covering your chest broke like the sea's
own banner, an edge-line of foam
        on a dark shore. I didn't want to wake you.

That day – years ago – we drove
by a row of cottages just above the beach.
        We didn't stay, or even stop,

but I can still see that line
of white clapboard boxes, barely big enough
        for a bed, each bearing a wooden sign

stenciled in green paint:
their names, which marched from *Aster*
        to *Zinnia*, a floral alphabet.

Traveling brings back every other summer
by the sea; our long, familiar conversation's
all *I remember* . . . and *Then* . . .

Memory seems a kind of shoreline,
the edge between sleep and the world.
We're never sure what we'll wake to —

what form the past, which has no boundaries,
has chosen for its intrusion into today,
or how our random memories will match

or collide. Remember Nantasket Beach,
on Labor Day, and how the Polish band
pumped out songs for the dancers,

old men and women bused
from the housing project? They held one another
as if they'd never let go,

and in the roofless bathhouse
you remembered your mother's angular
white sunglasses, the waxy pink sticks

for fixing Polaroids, I my father's Kodak
and old blue trunks; the details
don't matter, only the intimacy

they carry with them. Did I ever tell you
this? One summer vacation day it rained,
        and I must have been allowed out alone;

    I remember discovering a ladder
beside the shore, stark by the single
        breathing undulance that sea and sky made.

    A gull perched on top, triumphant
over a crust, his weight perched
        on one leg, then the other.

    Someone – a lifeguard? – must have lugged
the ladder out, abandoned it
        beside the water that was hurrying

    with the idea of storm. Nothing happened,
but the image is as clear as if
        I could mount the wooden steps.

    Every year we drive to the beach
as if we needed something huge
        but almost apprehensible,

    its only containment the line
that moves back and forth along blank sand,
        blurring the shore. Only a little

and indefinite border, the line
between then and now, the foamy edge-line
    where my ladder stood. Five years ago

    in that rented room I saw the shoreline break
above your heart, and that was all the dazzled coast
    I could want or hold. I could never remember

    so much alone. I think of that garden row
of cottages as a code for summer:
    the names of flowers marking, regular as iambs,

    the blank verse of a beach motel.
Not a place we'd ever want to stay
    (who could choose between *Marigold* and *Dahlia*?)

    but an image to keep, like a snapshot
acquiring the creased signatures
    of long attention. Not flowers,

    exactly, but words, all we can climb to,
stenciled on the clapboard along the waterfront:
    Cleome, Peony, Rose.

A Box of Lilies

I'm driving to work, late,
Tannhäuser on the tape player –

the skittering violins spiraling down
in their mortal pull

while the horns play out their grand theme:
the brilliant flourishes

before they fall. The strings plummet
again and again, and then the student

I'm meeting tells me he's fallen
in love, an old girlfriend

still lingering somewhere, the new sleek
with possibility. It doesn't matter

so much, he says, which he winds up loving;
his fall's "a beautiful event

with no significance." There's something bravura,
something nineteen in even saying it,

and I can't decide whether
to love or blame him, thinking of you,

how yesterday morning you set out
on a kind of going

we don't know the least thing about.
If I'd known you better I couldn't even

say this. This is what I imagine it's like,
Doug: once the mailman brought me

a box of lilies, by mistake
– shipping error, nursery packer's

benevolent whim? –
twenty-eight pale and armored hearts,

spiky as artichokes.
Nothing was labeled

but I could guess their intentions
by their heft; some were twinned,

even two-fisted, and the instructions plain:
Dig deeper than you need to,

fertilize with a little bone,
allow to remain undisturbed

for years. It took me a moment
to decide to keep them,

seasons to watch the stalks
thicken, the sure swell

of buds into waxy throats. My neighbor
leans down from her dizzying

third-floor porch, July,
toward the advent of trumpeting;

it's the beautiful event
in the garden she waits for,

and their fragrance goes hurrying
up; she's an interruption

en route to heaven. Last night
I burned two cones of incense

for you, one mesquite, one pine,
then I cleaned the guest room,

spreading a good quilt, arranging flowers.
There wasn't anything else

to do. Maybe dying's like being given
a box of what will be trumpets,

maybe it feels like a mistake,
and you plant them with all

the requisite attention
and wait for something

flaring. In the opera
Else renounces her life for love,

and the truth is her gesture matters
not because it's rare

but because there's nothing else to do
against the way these violins

seem to want to take us,
and will, though not before the horns

have played something unforgettable.
I don't know which I love better –

knowing the bulbs are there, this March,
scaled sleepers, or the brief July spangle

smudging our faces
with that golden lipstick.

I couldn't choose between them,
finally – the downward longing,

the trumpets in their brave clusters
year after year.

Paradise

James L. White, 1936–1981

I.

For you it's a hotel whose prime is long past,
so you don't have to anticipate anything.
All the clerks are beautiful,

and the old details there still:
portals of marble and uranium,
the tragic stones, carved with the forms

of flowers. You've probably named them:
Snowdrift, *First Time*, and one you call
Too Soon, and twisting among them

are the urgent torsos of gods
and horses. Jim, when I was a child
my parents used to take me

to a reconstructed temple,
a museum of broken friezes
where marble horses flared

their nostrils, reared back
as if in horror. For me
they were entirely without context,

the arching necks and huge blind eyes.
They looked as if they'd fling themselves
from their pedestals, contorted

but motionless, as men sometimes are,
in the ferocity of their repose.
I wish I'd known you. I imagine

an endless scrim of snow falls
outside your rented paradise,
though the banks grow no higher;

the downtown street's lovelier
as you grow more oblivious to it,
lost in the shy weight of an Indian boy

who's driven all night from a reservation
in South Dakota. He's going to stay
with you as long as you want. Tonight

you don't have to do anything,
only sleep a little
so that you can wake

to those astonishing flanks again.
Or, heaven is somewhere you don't need
to love anyone to feel all right.

2.

I read that blind children,
in a room painted deep blue,
became more tranquil, at ease,
as if what they could not see their way to
informed them. It's the same
with longing; finally it delivers
the object of desire not into our hands
but into the skin itself,
the bruising tattoo of *I want.*
It isn't even a question,
whether the subject or object
of desire is made more beautiful.

3.

I forget who told the story
about the garden for the blind,
how they'd learn to read the blue
and white rockets of delphinium,

the smolder of larkspur. It makes me
think of the men I used to meet
in the Victory Gardens' drifts
of plots and hedges, every alcove

alive with men until after dawn.
There are only a few I can remember
individually: the shirtless,
rippling boy in the painter's cap,

who was no boy at all,
his face preserved,
I guess, by the force of desire;
Rafael, the Puerto Rican exotic dancer

of the holy namesake, who became
a janitor in the baths,
a job for an angel of strong constitution;
the man who inhaled Freon all night

perched on an abandoned car seat
until he proclaimed himself Queen of the Fens
and fell over backward into the swamp.
Mostly they're vague, downtown lights

hazing above them as they paced
territories fenced by lathe and vine
and flowers that opened in the dark,
face up, throats wide to the moon.

Once the vice squad careened in,
headlights blaring at the only exit
to a little cul de sac and all of us leapt
terrified over the fences; I fell flat

in someone's lettuces, fleeing
the legislation of the body.
I want to defend us now,
our alliance of strangers,

but I don't have to explain it to you,
Jim, the tentative equality of the dark,
the pleasure of banning privacy,
touching anyone you wanted.

Some were too drunk to even stand,
and some just stood as if
they'd forgotten why they'd come.
I didn't know whose hands were whose;

the breathtaking fall from self
brought us farther into the garden,
blind readers who disappeared,
for a while, into the text.

In little clearings half a dozen men
become no one, and lost nothing.
I don't want to glorify this; the truth is
I wouldn't wish it on anyone,

though it is a blessing,
when all your life you've been told
you're no one, and you find a way
to be what you have been told,

and it's all right.

Maybe the dead look back
to the watered green silk of Earth
and name it Desire's Paradise,

and it must be hard for them,
formed as they were once in desire
and then over and over again.

Imagine it's longing that compels them
back to the world. You are snowdrift,
marble, classical in the stasis

in which you die into yourself again,
you feel so complete. Suppose
you have everything you need,

and then you realize what you lack
is need. And so I want you to wake again,
in longing, like the rest of us.

An Exhibition of Quilts

Necessity bloomed
into an exuberance of scraps,

with a rapturous language to match:
Feathered Star with Wild Goose Chase,

Princess Feather with Laurel Leaves,
Unnamed Pattern with Four Hearts.

Four Leaf Sprays and Four Pineapples.
The terms of their craft became landscape:

Prickly Path, Garden Maze,
Delectable Mountains.

Here everything's in motion
– Tumbling Blocks, Carpenter's Wheel –

and here, in one perfected yellow firmament,
are sixteen stars. Some shine

while others spin, since the maker's
shot five through with red plaid

pinwheel blades. The color's softened,
though it must have dazzled.

Which were her dresses,
which her husband's shirts?

Imagine her cutting apart
anything discarded

into squares and diamonds,
hurrying to fit them all in,

to get it right:
just beyond the day's veil,

her gospel's variable heavens.
Did she name it –

Whirling and Sleeping Stars,
Bethlehem in Broad Daylight?

Six Thousand Terra-cotta Men and Horses

Some farmers digging a well
five kilometers outside of Xian
broke through into the tomb,
and corrosive daylight fell

onto the necks of the horses,
the men's knotted hair,
after their dynasties in the dark.
The rooms had been studded

with torches of seals' fat,
so these eyes could, even buried,
give back light. What did the Emperor expect
when the oiled strips of silk

were consumed, smoldering?
The guards were individuated by the sculptors
– whoever *they* may have been –
down to an idiosyncratic chin, the detail

of a frown. This one 192 centimeters tall,
this 186. "Life-size," the catalog says.
Were they portraits, each someone recognized
once, lively and exact? They ranked

in squadrons, self-contained, at rest.
Did the chamber smell of scorched fat still?
And to bury even horses, these animated faces
who look eager to step out onto the wide,

grassy fields outside of Xian.
Their breed is still raised in Quinghai;
the colors incinerated by daylight
must have made them less alien, less formal.

Muscular, monumental as coffins set on end,
they are patient and eager at once,
poised as if beginning the first step
of a purely ornamental journey,

sun on their backs, nothing at stake,
the provinces united years ago
under the Emperor's beautiful will,
which came to nothing, though his horses stared

into the dark perfectly for two thousand years,
good-natured, their faces open and uncomplicated.

Pharoah's Daughter

The youth groups have all built floats
for the Fourth, and they parade
around and around the green;
    one club's done Pharoah's Daughter
        Finds Baby Moses in the Bullrushes.
        Reeds nailed to the flatbed rattle in the breeze

    while the handmaidens,
bored with their supporting roles,
fan themselves with peacock fans;
    in the blue paper swell cut
        to suggest the edge of the Nile
        a basket bobs a little as the truck bounces.

    In Vacation Bible School
the teacher used to show us pictures,
large, archaic things, from a folio
    I think called *Heroes of Bible Days*.
        They were colored like nothing else,
        lurid and a little unworldly,

    as if to suggest that Bible stories
took place on other planets;
Expulsion from the Garden,
    Joseph and His Coat of Many Colors
        might have been the names of so many stars.
        In the plate representing Pharoah's daughter,

the princess wore a white sheath
out of de Mille, and stood with her arms
thrown back in a theatrical pose
    of astonishment, though her eyes,
        outlined in streaks of kohl, were without surprise,
        simply acknowledging the inevitable arrival

    of the child she'd lift from the river.
We knew the boy would be safe from flood,
that the basket wouldn't snag in reeds;
    of course the mild current would always float him
        directly to the place where she was bathing.
        After the story we'd go to the table

    and draw, domesticating the exotic landscape
with our own personable, crayoned houses,
smoke twisting from our slanting chimneys.
    And each of us must have seen ourselves
        floating toward our mothers
        across a great distance, wondrous children,

    nearly unknowable. Someday our parents
would remember this about us:
that we traveled effortlessly,
    from far over water, an Egypt.
        We might be prophets. And then
        they might stand in that same pose of wonder,

like this high-school girl
chosen to portray her, bent in the same
expected attitude, wobbling a little
    as the truck slows down then lurches around the square,
        looking down, as she has for hours, into the basket
        in which she must imagine the form of her son.

Art Lessons

Bored with the still life her painting teacher
has composed – Oaxacan vase and copper
bowl, ragged sunflowers – my mother takes a long scrap
of watercolor paper and sketches whatever

emerges first: five Chinese horses,
each a few quick strokes of black ink.
Sun on their fluid and restless shoulders,
they seem to be running out her sudden rebellion.

She'll never paint like this again,
though the future doesn't matter now, not while these five
unstoppable animals – angry, perfect – derive
their strength from refusal and hurry off the page.

This isn't the lesson, the art teacher says,
and likes the painting anyway.

What if she'd continued that sheer
pleasure of refusal? No bruised years?
No little paintings of dark and smoldering
lilacs again and again, no vodka blurring

every afternoon to a troubled sheen?
No ice and then no glass: a disease.
Do I still believe that will alone
could have cured her? No one was home,

the world was slick, slurred. Everything's erased,
purposefully forgotten, impossible now to read.
Twenty years and still it's hard to breathe.
Could I let it in, all I still can't say?

That's the lesson: art is remembering, and turning away.
And the poem, refused, hurries off the page.

∽

The sets of slides my parents ordered
came wrapped in beautifully marbled
paper. Projected on our largest wall,
heat from the bulb rippling the image a little,

they offered worlds: a Rennaissance prince taut and alien
as his hawk; breath, in a Botticelli, blooming
into the millefiori of spring; Tintoretto's
palpable silk. When my father questioned Caravaggio's

– boy, was he, lavish hair and ambiguous smile framed
with grapeleaves? – I felt a sense of shame,
though I couldn't have said why.
I was to learn to name the art,

though the lesson ran deeper: this resonant intelligence,
this order, couldn't have come from people like us.

Didn't my parents see that?
We lived in a tract house, in Tucson,
Arizona, and I never heard anyone say *marbled*
or *Veronese*. I liked to stand

in the blasted grass of the backyard and study,
through my father's binoculars, the lavender bulk
of the mountains, the two sharp spires in the cleft
of one peak I thought of as a cathedral,

the shadowy place beneath them a door.
We'd take Sunday drives into the desert
and I saw remnants of some age grander than ours
in every wind-turned pinnacle,

as if the desert were classical,
demanding, framed. I wanted a world

constructed to be read, with an arch,
a tiny human figure in one corner to lend meaning
or scale. I didn't know art
was a world lost from the very beginning.

Now my mother's buried in a desert cemetery
irrigated into lawn, dominated
by the unforgettable outline of those mountains. My family
was a ruined gesture, a building that collapsed,

a few years after the art lessons,
into brutality and incoherence.
I wished myself no one's
son, uncompromised, airy as the monuments

magnified over the Naugahyde sofa, with no context
to embrace or erase. When I visited my father last

we drove to the Grand Canyon, with his new wife,
who has made him happy, and who narrated
every bit of landscape along the way.
And watching the foreign, arid cliffs, it was just the same,

as if I knew something my parents did not: what lay
around us had only been mistaken
for random stones. On a narrow spar over the canyon's
terrifying layers of color, I imagined

I was surrounded by ruins, doors
carved with the reliefs of their vanished inhabitants, doors
that yet would open, if only we could find them,
onto hidden chambers, the heartbreakingly

perfect collonades. Mother, Father,
listen: I was not born but made.

Cemetery Road

No one's been buried here for years,
on this hill above the landing strip
where lovers park, nights, and watch
what few small planes come and go –
maybe they love each other more,
witnessing these ordinary departures.

The evergreens are overgrown,
and the fence just a half-hearted gesture.
A few of the thinner slates –
dark today because it's rained
all morning, the sky hovering
at the edge of the second snow –

are smashed to pieces, a few
worn illegible. Those that stand
lean together in clusters,
stone archipelagos: *Glory*
with all her lamps shall burn . . .
Weep not for me,

I've quit my house of clay . . .
There's no narrative here –
only sentimental or cautionary verses
under the incised urns and willows,
the winged, weeping faces –
but I wanted to tell you this story:

Once I watched a psychic healer
draw pain out with such neutrality,
the way one pulls a weed sometimes,
finding it neither ugly nor beautiful,
merely noting its presence
where it isn't wanted. She told me

to imagine the garden within myself,
inviolable, and asked me to invite
into that brilliant shade
the women who had comforted me:
my grandmother with her red-lettered Bible,
my mother, on her good days.

And when she told me to divide
my own memory, and banish
the darker mother from the garden
I could not, because wherever she was
she was wrapped in a long healing,
and it was all right now.

But the psychic said,
"There is no time there.
All of the story happens at once;
bar her from the garden."
And when I finished the work,
the others who had come to be healed

held me while I was, for a time,
the purely vulnerable child again.
For days I felt furrowed and broken, and doubted
anything had happened at all
but the recurrence of my own grief.
I was wrong. I can't explain

how I know the dead continue,
how sometimes we carry them
and sometimes they propel themselves
into huge distances they understand
only a little better than we do.
And whatever injured me, Mother,

I want to tell you that childhood
is only a little blue grave now.
See, the boy beneath this slate
was born in 1798, and lived a single day,
but anyone walking here one hundred
and eighty-nine years has read his name.

And my own death is only a minor island,
and I will go past it, as you have.
Perhaps you prepare it already,
as one readies a room for guests:
here the clean linens, here
a porcelain bowl. Why did we ever stop

burying beloved objects, the things
found in tombs: toys, jewelry, roses?
What did that child have time
to love, descending into this chilly ground
before his mother's hands
even came into focus? And because

there is no time there,
you are also here with me,
ten years gone and walking
these ruts in the cemetery road,
the wind smelling of new snow
and October, gathering in a rush

under the stiff wings carved
on these blackened stones.
They lift you with such force and grace
I would never think of calling you back.
You are going forward into your future,
though perhaps what lies before you
can't be called that.

Against Paradise

Past the paperwhites breathing
at the window the fence pickets
syncopate my view, a rhythm
off a little, since the skewed posts
lean. It's a good fence,
sturdy despite its eccentricities,

like the neighborhood. The shadowed clapboard
of the apartment house next door's
gone glacial silver, and the pine
concentrates shadow at its core.
Twilight blues the spaces
between the pickets first;

the white spears shine
as footsteps shuffle past
– the paperboy, in his hooded sweatshirt
six-o'clock-in-December blue.
He bounces a kickball on its way
to flat, and in the hush that follows

a neighbor calls from her porch,
which blazes like an altar
of light bulbs and frozen laundry,
Johnny Boy, Johnny Boy,
a name she repeats mysteriously
and at regular intervals,

always in the same tone
which makes me suppose her cat
hasn't been home for years.
All we have of our neighbor's lives
is noise, and the stories we can make of it.
The woman next door goes by

singing, something like *Oh*
I'm going to the store
to buy some bread 'cause we don't have any
the roof of my apartment looks
so black . . . The words meander
around the scale like someone lost,

then fade. She'll be back soon,
wheeling a shopping cart from the grocery
as though it were a gift
she was bringing to the sure location
of a miracle, as though it were her job
to hurry home and continue

this composition of isolated events,
ordinary and fraught with evidence
of how things vanish before we're ready
– the ghost of Johnny Boy
stalking the winter birds – how light
makes things look a certain way

once. Another song to no audience,
then the red cart
abandoned on a sidewalk ranged
with snow, gleaming in last light
as if someone has polished it spotless.
Galaxies of frozen breath,

these narcissus cluster.
The fence literally glows.
I couldn't have imagined that.
Its shadows spike the snow;
I couldn't love any world but this.
It's almost dark. *Johnny Boy.*

EARLY POEMS

I started writing poetry when I was sixteen or seventeen, and worked with some intensity from then until my first full-length book, *Turtle, Swan*, was published by Godine when I was 33, in 1987. I'd been publishing in literary journals, and three chapbooks – now long gone – had found their way into print, but the majority of those early poems never appeared in a collection. This spring I read through lots of this old work, with an eye toward finding some early poems to include here, and I have to report that it wasn't a lot of fun to do so. I'm remembering a day when I was a first grader in Memphis, and for some reason I was allowed to go up into the hot attic of our smallish bungalow-style house. There were trunks, and old things put away – my father's navy uniform, a fruitcake tin full of old photographs. Best of all, there was my stuffed tiger: a little worn, friendly, with green glass eyes. I'd forgotten that I ever had a tiger, or rather he'd simply just been set aside; another room of the house meant another ancillary zone of memory. Finding my tiger meant, to my young self, that suddenly I had a history, a past; it was a great surprise, at six, to discover the material evidence of a former self.

Which is pretty much what those old poems are. Those nights when I'd come home from work and write I was practicing the art, pursuing a vivid image or a potent phrase; I was putting in my time learning the vocabulary and manners of the period style of the day; I was apprenticing. These poems seem to me to have been written by someone else, more or less, though I was interested to see what the poems revealed – how little self-awareness was evident, and how much anger, guilt and sorrow were acted out without the writer quite knowing what he was up to. Of course great poems can be built upon those emotions, but it helps to know you're feeling them. I was trying hard, as young poets sometimes do, to sound like the writers I loved.

It's only around 1980 that I start to recognize the man who's speaking. That's one thing I liked about doing this reading, seeing what have become familiar gestures or vocal strategies emerge – suddenly there I am, becoming me. This seems mysterious – wasn't I always myself? Yes and no. Maybe the turn of voice was there, the habit of speech or the manner of thinking, but here it is in this poem or that appearing on the page, and thus in some way concretizing a self: a manner of speaking, a means of making meaning. The poems gathered here are from the early eighties, at a time when I had just moved out of a heterosexual marriage and was discovering the terms of a more authentic life. I can see a style emerging in them, but also ways of thinking, rehearsals for concerns and questions that will be given a larger form later on. I haven't revised them, at least not by adding anything or rearranging, but I have allowed myself the opportunity to trim them back a bit, throwing out extra words or weak lines I didn't notice at the time. In this way the poems are more taut and lively than they were in the condition I found them, but I don't see the point in publishing something you can easily improve just out of allegiance to the past. Revising them entirely would be another matter, and would feel dishonest, but I felt I could prune these back without doing damage to the poems' orig-

inary impulses – and in the process make a better experi-
ence for the reader. I've kept the selection brief, as I can't
see why anyone would want to read a lot of this stuff, but
nonetheless I hope there's pleasure in it, and perhaps
something intriguing about watching a younger poet build-
ing foundations for inquiries and outpourings to come.

MARK DOTY
2011

Plan 9

"The future's where we'll spend the rest of our lives,"
says the narrator in *Plan 9 from Outer Space,*
some "psychic" hired for the day to lend the tone of newsreel

to this thriller's pieplate flying saucers
wobbling across the screen's rectangle of sky.
The aliens have a plan: they'll shoot electrode rays

into the graces of the newly dead and effect
a resurrection. Before anyone's had a chance to forget them,
the dead are awake, spreading their capes

and lurking beside cardboard tombs in a cemetery
in the San Fernando Valley. "You earth people are all idiots,"
the spaceman mutters. The hero swells

and threatens, "Now hold it a minute,
buster. . ." Though I love the bravado, human bluster
that carries us through, tonight I couldn't agree

with the alien more, no matter how silly his satin suit
with the appliquéd lightning is. This hokum's
        strangely true:
the past is insistent,

and like this movie's ghouls
doesn't really *do* anything,
just lurks in the inevitable dead trees,

a phantom whose intentions we can't guess.
What I'd choose to erase
seems to replay like these shoddy special effects.

I hate memory. Though I know I owe it
the hope of order, I'm tired of craning my neck up
to the flare or dark

of the screen, tired of being determined
the way a day's colored by clouds,
the sky's decisions. The weather

of these zombies is black and white,
the lightning making their hearts crackle
under a night threaded by the silver flash

of saucers. They lurch in the dark
with no location in mind they'd call a future.
At least the spacemen can escape

– those slick aluminum ships, however flimsy,
do lift off from earth to unscathed ethers,
leaving no tracks in the air.

New Stars

Nearly at the end of a long, sad marriage
you hesitate on the steps of the planetarium,
buy a ticket, enter. The black projector,
a fly's head of dials and lenses, swivels
in the center of the room. "The Beginning,"
the show is called. Soon you notice
that the room has darkened and everyone
around you has stopped speaking;
even the children are quiet. Projected clouds
begin to swirl across the dome. You think
you would like to forget yourself now, forget her,
the tenuous connection between you, and simply
become lost in the convincing illusion of storm.
Then there are stars: cool, incredibly numerous
almost close enough to touch, as if every night
you'd lain on your back in wet grass had suddenly
been brought to some higher power of resolution.
You try to pay attention to the wavering pointer
and soothing voice that want to tell you about gods,
hunters, a swan, all the old patterns
of the summer night, but you find yourself drifting,
more interested in the fixed, unblinking scatter
in which nothing familiar can finally be read.
When the stars begin to revolve, you feel as though
your seat were flying upward. Your fixed point
of view vanishes; you are reeling, breathless,
as the narrator asks you to go back toward the beginning
a distant explosion that still fills space with static.
The voice tells you the age of light

from the Pleiades; that hot cup of jewels
may have been dead since men and women
first climbed the rubble slopes of Olduvai.
And there is so much light from still further,
sliding into red shift, the spectrum's polite way
of saying goodbye. Think of the telescope on Palomar,
how it admits a million times more light
than the eye. Although you're very tired,
there is still something you love about the stars,
harder now to explain than it once was:
once you could lie beneath any one of them
and feel that it observed you and oddly concerned you.
Now you know the choice was yours, and arbitrary;
you drew a chalkline from yourself to any bright pole
and called it permanent. Now you are a fleck
in the bright dust of night sky, alone,
and about to be strangely happy.

1980

The forecast snow's nowhere in sight.
I'd wanted our street filled with that visible silence.
Only the paperwhites' albino stars in the window,
and outside, the grass grown intricate with frost,
secrets without intimacies. In the mornings
the Laotian children walk to school together,
eldest leading, and stop beside our crabapple.
The uninterrupted bells of their voices
rise to the window of the bathroom where I lean
into the steamy, unyielding oval of the mirror. Half-asleep,
I imagine us on a pier beside a dozen bobbing boats,
barely moored. Names, fitness for travel unknown,
no predictions of the weather. Looking at the brilliant
or battered hulls, which do you choose?

Walking down the stairs, I see a single planet
framed in the landing window, repeat a few phrases
to steady myself: *It's just you and me now,*
Skyrocket. The magic of denial is no longer ours to use.
Another year . . . At breakfast, I tear a chrysanthemum apart
in a cup: the odor of petals, green-tinged,
rises in the steam of the tea. Reading the leaves:
No use baling a burning boat.
Cultivate solitary pastimes.
You will take a journey over water.

At the gas station, the attendant boy's swathed
in a hooded blue sweatshirt, his breath steaming
like a Magellanic cloud. The pump

stops at 19.80, bell behind iced glass
ringing the decade. A bell means something's over:
remember time to come in from recess,
time to wake up? The attendant wipes his hands
against his blue pockets, tosses back his hair,
counts out my change. He stands
so firmly in his own life it frightens me.

Leinster

Driving a rented car
   in that poor, green country
     – all piety,

utterly faithless –
   we'd turn on the road
     least known or likely,

ramblings that led
   to boredom, sometimes,
     a constant struggle for petrol,

and discoveries: Aherlow,
   pale tinker kids peering
     from a wagon's smoky dark,

a backroads crossing's
   hot scones, berries
     preserved thick and sugared

from laden canes,
   strong tea. A flowerpot
     in the window rimmed

by snail shells,
   whorls of reticent,
     summer colors;

after the baker gave us directions
    to the strand
        we picked them up,

one at a time,
    two handfuls
        already fading.

Another wrong turn:
    a picnic on Mt. Leinster,
        crooked fields

cropped by stone,
    small clouds of wool
        drifting loose on hedge

and thorn branch.
    A barrow of bread,
        Amsterdam cheese,

Cork sherry,
    green mustard
        from Paris – the familiar

marriage of poverty and glamour.
    We lay on our backs
        on a small blanket

and damp grass
    while a thin rain
        masked the peak.

I forgot the fog of whiskey,
    your growing need
        my reasonable fears;

you forgot, or seemed to,
    my wilful attraction to others
        and my real sin,

the love of your weakness.
    We gave up the fear
        of being stranded

in that country's
    collective broken heart
        and incomprehensible English.

Though the figure
    of our disaster
        already loomed

like a landscape
    in uncertain climate,
        though we approached,

steadily, as if powerless,
    the refusals that would
        leave us faded

like the shells we carried home,
    we were not sorry.
        A postcard happiness

with a brief vocabulary:
    foreign roads,
        a faith in better weather,

an immoral denial
    that pleased us:
        a shred of belief

our outcome
    would be other
    than it was:

strange tenderness,
    the loss and passport
        any refusal is.

Had we been only tourists,
    all our lives we could
        have loved one another.

We gave ourselves up
    to an inadequate language
        of small times: green walls,

new bread, Sunday morning light
    in a field on the other side
        of the world.

Alexander Nevsky

Because of the storm warning, only three of us
are scattered in the theater when the Cyrillic titles
sputter and flash. In the lake's severe light,
the subtitles vanish into day:

this print of a print's so poor
blonde Russian princes are white figures
on white ground. Odd to think these actors
formed in heroic poses,

rousing the sleeping peasants, all dead now.
When the Teutonic invasion's repelled,
the lake breaks apart; the intruders, masked
in helmets marked by beak or iron claw,

tumble into gaps in the ice
whose surface resembles the film itself:
black form beneath pure white segments of light.
But the fallen of Novgorod

lie sprawled on more solid ice,
a field of dying reaching all the way
to a distant cyc. They lift themselves
as if performing an asana; as one sinks

another rises, and each groans a word
the subtitles – visible now
against the harsh gray of ice –
don't even try to translate: a syllable

thick with the wonder of still being,
even knocked flat on the ice-field
of the mortally wounded, able to lift
only a few inches toward the air

brimming with lights and monumental,
Stalinist clouds, to hold the eye open
an instant, amazed. . . .
Outside, it's snowing harder

than ever, the streets become frames
the editor left out, scenes in which
it simply snows and snow, white substance
and black gaps like the bottomless lake

breaking apart. A pair of girls
– music students? – walk under
a streetlamp beneath the spread dark
of an umbrella, singing in clear,

high sopranos that might be the song
of the snow itself. White figures,
white ground, they seem about to be lost,
though perhaps identity's multiple,

collaborative. Though the flakes multiply,
a rhythm no one could freeze or precisely name,
it is one storm, and their voices spiral up
through its immense weight

untranslatable as the soldiers' astonished word.

January, Waking

Beneath the covers I look up
into green voices, small eclipses

focused between leaves,
a sunlit rhythm spilled from beak

and throat. You're making coffee,
playing an album of birds.

They seem to flash wing and plume
above these sleep-heavy blankets,

a trill and pause unrepeatable
as the pattern of snow falling

on the street and lawn.
I practice ornithology:

here's a Summer Chalcedony,
Clouded July, a Blue Nicaragua,

a Paraguay. In your concert
the kettle bangs against the stove,

the burner bursts into a blue nest;
you end with a coda of footsteps

mounting the stairs, wake me,
a little while, to every branch

in the world laden. How simple:
thaw the air and it sings.

Single

I live on a row of student apartments,
in a turn of the century house partitioned
into clusters of a few rooms, lit
at night like a cruise liner carrying
a choir of stereos. In the morning
light through east windows fills this space
with an almost visible tenderness. So human
a quality to assign these waves or streams
of particles that fall everywhere, indifferent. . .
One would almost feel regarded by the world
were the day any less ordinary:
a few cyclists moving in and out of traffic,
the early September leaves full-veined and heavy,
the new black station – "soul of the city" -
coolly quoting the odds of storm,
horoscopes: *Your secret: you need to love*
and be loved more than most. Keep moving.
I read the personals: mutually fulfilling relationship,
prefer daytime hours. SWF, GWM, BiBF, SDM:
the acronyms blur, an alphabet of need.
An engine grinds, turns over, a mailbox clanks
as someone lifts the lid for a bill, a love letter.
Wind parts the too-long grass, the telephone
silent as a confessor. The end of summer,
cat at the door. This easy, to be single,
the spin and sing of an approaching bike
humming into the sunlight.

Three Sundays, a Saturday, Roses, Photographs

Sunday after you've gone I photograph
first a rose, then the empty bed's
symmetry of pillows, tousled sheets,
the chair where you piled your clothes.
I walk the hill from the Art Center
to the amphitheatre's cluster
of benches, enameled green,
beautiful in neglected order.
The pond's skimmed by new ice,
sudden geometry. The rose garden's
rows and rows of bundled stalks
are tied and clipped. On a white pole,
a warning sign: *Let no one say, and say it*
to your shame, that all was beauty here
before you came. No one will:
I'm a flowering I never earned
or imagined, late November bloom.
I duck into the museum to warm up;
a string trio's playing Arensky,
music I don't recognize, do.
The violin dives to someplace
I didn't know could be touched.

Sunday after you've gone
your photograph shines from the pillow
where you placed it while I hunted
keys, gloves. Leaning on black sleeves
on the roof of the car, your face,
radiant mask of what you've just said.

Saturday you emerge from the department store
with a long florist's box. At first I think
Who are they for? We've declared
this Christmas: lights, a paper circus
(you were a plate-spinner once, white-faced)
a toy rocking horse like one you rode
as a child in Spain till his ankles weakened
and you could only stroke wooden flanks,
set his brave soul galloping. . .
The roses breathe, fill
so much space; the trio of white rooms
recedes into a warm void
even the violins can't touch. A touch,
a little gravity: the secret of perpetual motion.
Sunday after you've gone the radio delivers
some Spanish *Gloria.* I'm speaking
to the door you've walked through, thank you,
the appreciative morning, thank you, the flock
of grateful things you've touched.
My face rests on my own sleeve: cotton
imbued with you, scent and dye
soaked even into the fibers. Look,
simply: camera face-up
on the table, the bowl of roses'
blushed and burnished grammar,
these candles you've given me,
shafts of potential light
These are the wonders of the world.

Acknowledgments

Acknowledgment is made to the following publications, in which some of the poems in this book first appeared.

Agni Review: "Playland," "Six Thousand Terra-cotta Men and Horses"; *Calliope*: "Anna Karenina"; *Crazyhorse*: "Independence Day," "Turtle, Swan," "Beginners," "Cemetery Road"; *Dog Pond Review*: "The Ancient World"; *Fiction International*: "Three Sundays, A Saturday, Roses, Photographs"; *Green Mountains Review*: "A Box of Lilies," *Indiana Review*: "63rd Street Y"; *Iowa Review*: "Gardenias"; *Ironwood*: "For Louise Michel"; *Mississippi Review*: "Paragon Park," "Late Conversation," "The Garden of the Moon"; *Missouri Review*: "In the Form of Snow"; *New England Review*: "1980"; *New England Review and Breadloaf Quarterly*: "Pharoah's Daughter"; *Nimrod*: "Horses"; *Ploughshares*: "A Replica of the Parthenon," "Tiara"; *Poet & Critic*: "New Stars"; *Poetry*: "Shaker Orchard," "Ararat," "The Death of Antinoüs"; *Poetry Miscellany*: "A Collection of Minerals"; *Poetry Northwest*: "Charlie Howard's Descent," "Hair," "Adonis Theater"; *Quarterly West*: "Single"; *Slant*: "La Belle et la Bête"; *Tendril*: "January, Waking"; *Texas Review*: "Sideshow"; *The Yale Review*: "Harbor Lights."

"Gardenias," "Latin Dances," and "Late Conversation" appeared in *New American Poets of the 80's*, Wampeter Press, 1985. "Turtle, Swan" appeared in *The Pushcart Prize XI, Best of the Small Presses*, Pushcart Press/Penguin Books, 1986. "Charlie Howard's Descent" was awarded the Theodore Roethke Prize from Poetry Northwest for 1986. "Tiara" appeared in *Poets for Life: Seventy-Six Poets Respond to AIDS*, Crown Books, 1989. "Cemetery Road" appeared in *Spreading the Word*, Bench Press, 1990.

The author would also like to thank the Massachusetts Artists Foundation, the Vermont Council on the Arts, and the National Endowment for the Arts for their generous assistance.

About the Author

Since the publication of his first volume of verse, Turtle, Swan, *in 1987, Mark Doty, born in 1953, has been recognized as one of the most accomplished poets in America. Hailed for his elegant, intelligent verse, Doty has often been compared to James Merrill, Walt Whitman, and C. P. Cavafy.*

The recipient of numerous grants and fellowships, Doty has also won a number of prestigious literary awards, including the Whiting Writers' Award, the T. S. Eliot Prize, the National Poetry Series, the Los Angeles Times *Book Award, the National Book Critics' Circle Award, the PEN/Martha Albrand Award for First Non-fiction, and the National Book Award.*

He has written nine books of poetry and five books of non-fiction, including the acclaimed memoir Dog Years *(2007). A long-time resident of Provincetown, Massachusetts, he now lives in New York City and in The Springs, New York, on the eastern end of Long Island. He teaches at Rutgers University in New Jersey.*

A Note on the Type

Paragon Park *has been set in FF Scala, a type designed by Martin Majoor in 1989. Derived in part from historic faces like Bembo and Fournier, Scala was intended to improve upon weaknesses the designer perceived in types then available. The result was a type with low contrast and solid serifs. FontShop released the roman and italic fonts two years later, but it was only when a companion sans serif family was released in 1993 that the types really became popular with designers. Majoor has continued to develop the family, creating a spectrum of weights and a group of display faces called Scala Jewels. ❧ The display type is William Morris's Golden type, first used by the Kelmscott Press in 1892 and based on the types of Nicolas Jenson.*

DESIGN & COMPOSITION BY CARL W. SCARBROUGH